1

Writing to Communicate

Paragraphs

Cynthia A. Boardman

Spring International Language Center
University of Arkansas at Fayetteville

PEARSON
Longman

D1410450

Writing to Communicate 1: Paragraphs

Pearson Education, 10 Bank Street, White Plains, NY 10606

Staff credits: The people who made up the *Writing to Communicate 1: Paragraphs* team, representing editorial, production, design, and manufacturing, are Danielle Belfiore, Wendy Campbell, Ann France, Laura Le Dréan, Françoise Leffler, Edith Pullman, Paula Van Ells, and Dorothy E. Zemach.

Cover photo: Momatiuk-Eastcott/Corbis
Text art and composition: Carlisle Publishing Services
Text font: 12.5/14 Minion
Illustrations: Steve Schulman

Photo credits: p. xv © Richard T. Nowitz/Corbis; **p. 1** Tatiana Morozova/Shutterstock; **p. 2** © Jon Arnold Images/Alamy; **p. 14** Mary Evans Picture Library/Alamy; **p. 16** Mary Evans Picture Library/Alamy; **p. 18** (first) Hulton Archive/Getty Images, (second) Dave M. Benett/Getty Images, (third) Time Life Pictures/Getty Images, (fourth) Tekee Tanwar/Getty Images, (fifth) © Peter Turnley/Corbis, (sixth) © Tim Graham/Corbis, (seventh) © Alessandro Della Valle/Keystone/epa/Corbis, (eighth) © Bettmann/Corbis; **p. 25** rubberball/Getty Images; **p. 37** © Sunnyart/Dreamstime.com; **p. 38** © David Lyons/Alamy; **p. 40** (first) Suhendri Utet/Shutterstock, (second) © Ace Stock Limited/Alamy, (third) Amanda Rohde/istockphoto; **p. 46** (first) © SuperStock/SuperStock, (second) © Ned Frisk Photography/Corbis, (third) © Bloomimage/Corbis, (fourth) © Stockbyte/Alamy, (fifth) © Index Stock Imagery, Inc., (sixth) Darko Novakovic/Shutterstock; **p. 48** © Reuters/Corbis; **p. 56** David Woolley/Getty Images; **p. 57** Mary Evans Picture Library/Alamy; **p. 65** Hu Xiao Fang/Shutterstock; **p. 66** Rubberball Productions; **p. 73** © Corbis; **p. 76** © Corbis; **p. 82** ThinkStock LLC/Index Stock Imagery; **p. 95** Thomas M. Perkins/Shutterstock; **p. 96** Sandra Behne/Getty Images; **p. 100** (first) Andy Lyons/Getty Images, (second) Justin Sullivan/Getty Images, (third) Paul Buck/Getty Images; **p. 104** © Atlantide Phototravel/Corbis; **p. 113** © Reed Saxon/Associated Press; **p. 115** Walt Disney Pictures/The Kobal Collection; **p. 116** 20th Century Fox/Paramount/The Kobal Collection

Library of Congress Cataloging-in-Publication Data
Boardman, Cynthia A.
    Writing to communicate 1: paragraphs / Cynthia A. Boardman.
        p. cm.
    ISBN 0-13-614191-9 (student book: alk. paper)—ISBN 0-13-614192-7 (answer key: alk. paper)

    1. English language—Textbooks for foreign speakers. 2. English language—Paragraphs—Problems, exercises etc. 3. English language—Rhetoric—Problems, exercises etc. 4. Academic writing—Problems, exercises etc. I. Title. II. Title: Writing to communicate one.
    PE1128.B5937 2008
    808'.042—dc22

                                                    2007017342

ISBN-10: 0-13-614191-9
ISBN-13: 978-0-13-614191-4

Printed in the United States of America
2 3 4 5 6 7 8 9 10—VHG—11 10 09 08

DEDICATION

I dedicate this book to my colleagues and to my students at UC Berkeley Extension's English Language Program in San Francisco from 1991 through 2003. It was my honor and pleasure to know them all, and it breaks my heart that we were forced to close.

ACKNOWLEDGMENTS

First and foremost, I'd like to thank Laura Le Dréan of Pearson Education for her encouragement and support in getting this series, in general, and this book, in particular, off the ground. Her comments and suggestions on the first drafts of *Writing to Communicate 1* were invaluable in shaping the organization and content of the book. I owe Françoise Leffler, my development editor at Pearson, many, many thanks for her efforts to make my chapters into a cohesive book. Not enough praise can be given to the "behind the scenes" people at Pearson without whom this book would be a mess! These wonderful people are Danielle Belfiore, Wendy Campbell, Ann France, Edith Pullman, and Paula Van Ells. Finally, I thank Pearson for assigning Dorothy E. Zemach to oversee the project in the final stages. Her skills in teaching English, her editing and design knowledge, and her steadfast support were very much appreciated.

I also wish to thank the reviewers for their insights and suggestions, many of which were incorporated into this book: **Meghan Ackley**, University of Texas, Austin, TX; **Kimberly Bayer-Olthoff**, Hunter College IELI, New York, NY; **Michael Climo**, Antelope Valley College, Lancaster, CA; **Sally Gearhart**, Santa Rosa Junior College, Santa Rosa, CA; **Kate Johnson**, Intensive English Institute, Union County College, Elizabeth, NJ; **Laura Shier**, Portland State University, Portland, OR; **Dina Paglia**, Hunter College IELI, New York, NY; **Laurette Poulos Simmons**, Howard Community College, Columbia, MD; **Joanna Vaughn**, Language Studies International, Berkeley, CA.

Jia Frydenberg also provided feedback on the later drafts, and I thank her for her willingness to read and comment on each chapter. I'd also like to thank **Martha Compton**, friend for over 25 years and amateur photographer, who traveled from her home in Santiago, Chile, to Valparaiso in order to get a picture of that beautiful city and its funiculars.

Finally, I am indeed indebted to the many students I have had throughout my teaching career. It is they, after all, who have helped me hone my skills in teaching writing to the point where I feel I have something to offer to novice and not-so-novice ESL/EFL teachers alike.

Cynthia A. Boardman

CONTENTS

To the Teacher xi

To the Student xiii

INTRODUCTION: WRITING IN ENGLISH xv

PART I: PARAGRAPH ORGANIZATION 1

CHAPTER 1 THE TOPIC SENTENCE 2
Predicting Personality

Vocabulary Builder 2

Writing Focus 4

    Paragraph Organization in English 4

    The Topic Sentence 5

    More about Controlling Ideas 7

Structure and Mechanics 8

    Simple Sentences 8

    Paragraph Format 9

    Writing a Title 10

Writing to Communicate 11

    The Writing Process, Part 1 11

        Step 1: Understanding the Assignment 11

        Step 2: Brainstorming 11

        Step 3: Organizing Your Ideas 11

    Your Turn 12

    Paragraph Checklist 13

    Writing to Communicate . . . More 13

CHAPTER 2 SUPPORTING SENTENCES 14
Analyzing Personality

Vocabulary Builder 14

Writing Focus 15

    Supporting Sentences 15

        Major Supporting Sentences 16

        Minor Supporting Sentences 16

        Using Connectors with Major Supporting Sentences 20

Structure and Mechanics 21

    Parts of Speech 21

    Lists and Commas 21

Writing to Communicate 22
    The Writing Process, Part 2 22
        Step 4: Writing 22
    Your Turn 22
    Paragraph Checklist 24
    Writing to Communicate...More 24

CHAPTER 3   THE CONCLUDING SENTENCE 25
Family and Personality

Vocabulary Builder 25

Writing Focus 26
    The Concluding Sentence 26
        Types of Concluding Sentences 27
        Transitions Used in Concluding Sentences 28

Structure and Mechanics 29
    Simple Sentences 29
    Compound Sentences 30
    Combining Simple Sentences with the Same Subject 31

Writing to Communicate 32
    The Writing Process, Part 3 32
        Step 4: Writing 32
        Step 5: Rewriting 33
        Step 6: Writing the Final Draft 33
    Your Turn 33
    Paragraph Checklist 34
    Writing to Communicate...More 34

PART I: BRINGING IT ALL TOGETHER 35
    Reviewing Terms 35
    Reviewing Ideas 35
    Error Analysis 36

PART II: BASIC TYPES OF PARAGRAPHS 37

CHAPTER 4   DESCRIPTIVE PARAGRAPHS 38
Describing People

Vocabulary Builder 38

Writing Focus 40
    Descriptive Paragraphs 40
        Prepositions of Place in Descriptive Paragraphs 41

Structure and Mechanics 44
    Using Adjectives. 44
    The Order of Adjectives before Nouns 45

Writing to Communicate 46
    Your Turn. 46
    Paragraph Checklist. 47
    Writing to Communicate...More 47

CHAPTER 5   NARRATIVE PARAGRAPHS 48
Telling Stories

Vocabulary Builder. 48

Writing Focus. 49
    Narrative Paragraphs 49
        Transitions in Narrative Paragraphs 50

Structure and Mechanics 50
    Complex Sentences 50
        Verb Tenses with Dependent Clauses of Time. 51

Writing to Communicate 53
    Your Turn. 53
    Paragraph Checklist. 55
    Writing to Communicate...More 55

CHAPTER 6   EXPOSITORY PARAGRAPHS 56
Communicating

Vocabulary Builder. 56

Writing Focus 57
    Expository Paragraphs. 57
        Transitions in Expository Paragraphs 57

Structure and Mechanics 58
    Using Transitions 58

Writing to Communicate 60
    Your Turn. 60
    Paragraph Checklist. 61
    Writing to Communicate...More 61

PART II: BRINGING IT ALL TOGETHER 62

    Reviewing Terms 62
    Reviewing Ideas 62
    Error Analysis 63

PART III: CHARACTERISTICS OF GOOD WRITING 65

CHAPTER 7 UNITY 66
Experiencing Emotions

Vocabulary Builder 66

Writing Focus 67
    Unity 67

Structure and Mechanics 70
    Combining Sentences 70

Writing to Communicate 71
    Your Turn 71
    Paragraph Checklist 72
    Writing to Communicate...More 72

CHAPTER 8 COHERENCE 73
Learning about Family History

Vocabulary Builder 73

Writing Focus 74
    Coherence 74
        Descriptive Paragraphs and Space Order 75
        Narrative Paragraphs and Time Order 76
        Expository Paragraphs and Logical Order 77
        Coherence and Connectors 78

Structure and Mechanics 79
    Avoiding Fragments 79

Writing to Communicate 80
    Your Turn 80
    Paragraph Checklist 81
    Writing to Communicate...More 81

CHAPTER 9 COHESION 82
Dating and Marrying

Vocabulary Builder 82

Writing Focus 83
    Cohesion 83
        Connectors 84
        The Definite Article 84
        Personal Pronouns 85
        Demonstrative Pronouns 85

Structure and Mechanics 86
    Being Consistent with Person and Number 86
        Personal Pronouns 86
        Demonstrative Pronouns 88

Writing to Communicate 89
    Your Turn 89
    Paragraph Checklist 90
    Writing to Communicate…More 90

PART III: BRINGING IT ALL TOGETHER 91
    Reviewing Terms 91
    Reviewing Ideas 91
    Error Analysis 93

PART IV: OTHER TYPES OF PARAGRAPHS 95

CHAPTER 10 PROCESS 96
Playing a Sport

Vocabulary Builder 96

Writing Focus 99
    Process 99
        Transitions in a Process Paragraph 99

Structure and Mechanics 101
    Using the Imperative 101
    Using the Negative Imperative 101
    The Imperative and Dependent Clauses 101

Writing to Communicate 102
    Your Turn 102
    Paragraph Checklist 103
    Writing to Communicate…More 103

CHAPTER 11 REASONS AND RESULTS 104
Exercising

Vocabulary Builder 104

Writing Focus 106
    Explaining with Reasons and Results 106
        Giving Reasons 106
        Giving Results 107

Structure and Mechanics 108
    Connectors for Reason and Result 108
    Reviewing Types of Sentences 110

Simple Sentences 110
Compound Sentences 110
Complex Sentences 110

Writing to Communicate 111
Your Turn 111
Paragraph Checklist 112
Writing to Communicate...More 112

CHAPTER 12 OPINION 113
Discussing Movies

Vocabulary Builder 113

Writing Focus 115
Opinion Paragraphs 115
Using Examples 115
Using Reasons 116
Transitions for Opinion Paragraphs 116
Transitions of Opinion 117
Transitions for Order of Importance 117

Structure and Mechanics 117
Avoiding Run-On Sentences 117

Writing to Communicate 119
Your Turn 119
Paragraph Checklist 119
Writing to Communicate...More 119

PART IV: BRINGING IT ALL TOGETHER 120

Reviewing Terms 120
Reviewing Ideas 120
Error Analysis 121

APPENDIX 1: GOING THROUGH THE WRITING PROCESS 122

APPENDIX 2: COMMON CONNECTORS 124

APPENDIX 3: A COMPLETE PARAGRAPH CHECKLIST 127

APPENDIX 4: COMPUTER FORMATTING 128

APPENDIX 5: PARAGRAPH EVALUATION 131

APPENDIX 6: SUGGESTED CORRECTION SYMBOLS 132

INDEX 135

TO THE TEACHER

About the Series

Welcome to the first book in a new series developed from *Writing to Communicate: Paragraphs and Essays, Second Edition*. This three-book series covers paragraphs, paragraphs and essays, and essays and short research papers.

This first book, **Writing to Communicate 1**, concentrates on teaching students to write well-developed paragraphs. The intended proficiency level is high elementary to low intermediate.

The second book, **Writing to Communicate 2**, will essentially be a third edition to *Writing to Communicate, Second Edition*, and will do what it has always done: take intermediate and high-intermediate students through the detailed step-by-step process of turning a paragraph into an essay. Part I of this book, however, has been shortened and is now a review of the paragraph.

The third book in the series, **Writing to Communicate 3**, is intended for low-advanced students. While it reviews the writing process and personal essays, the major focus of this book is to provide guidelines on research and documentation, resulting in documented essays and research papers.

Foundation and Organization

The methodology that was put forth in *Writing to Communicate, Second Edition*, teaching writing through **recursiveness** and **scaffolding**, is held throughout this book. A recursive method of teaching is essential to the process of writing. Scaffolding, taking students from the known to the unknown, allows students to slowly build on their knowledge. Both are paramount to teaching students how to write in academic English.

Writing to Communicate 1 was designed as a practical approach to the teaching of academic writing. Learning the concepts of good writing is not dependent on proficiency level because the concepts are not based on language. Rather, they are cognitive and can be understood in that sense. It is, however, essential to keep the language in the explanations and models accessible to students so that they aren't distracted by vocabulary items they don't know.

Writing to Communicate 1 is divided into four parts:

- **Part 1: Paragraph Organization**, which covers the topic sentence, the body, and the concluding sentence
- **Part 2: Basic Types of Paragraphs**, which deals with descriptive, narrative, and expository writing
- **Part 3: Characteristics of Good Writing**, which focuses on the concepts of unity, coherence, and cohesion
- **Part 4: Other Types of Paragraphs**, which discusses process, reason and result, and opinion

These patterns were chosen with an eye toward grammatical simplicity for the target proficiency level.

Each part has three chapters, which in turn are divided into four sections.

Chapter Format

The first section of the chapter is a **Vocabulary Builder**. This section focuses not only on words that students may need to understand the models but also, and more importantly, that they will need when they write their own paragraphs.

Writing Focus is the second section of each chapter. In this section are explanations of the principles of writing, model paragraphs, and practice exercises. Words in the model paragraphs that may be unknown to students but that are not important for their writing are glossed.

Structure and Mechanics is the third section of every chapter. The types of sentences (simple, compound, and complex) are the crux of this section. A few problematic grammar points that relate to the particular writing focus for that chapter are also covered.

Finally, the last section of each chapter, **Writing to Communicate**, leads students through the writing process as it provides topics for students to discuss and write about. This section also has a Paragraph Checklist and topics for further writing practice.

Appendices

Writing to Communicate 1 has six appendices—*Going Through the Writing Process, Common Connectors, A Complete Paragraph Checklist, Computer Formatting, Paragraph Evaluation,* and *Suggested Correction Symbols*—that may be photocopied and distributed for classroom use. There is also an index of terminology used in this book for easy reference.

Answer Key

An Answer Key with suggested answers to the exercises is published in a separate booklet.

TO THE STUDENT

Students in colleges and universities write for many reasons. They write e-mails and letters because they want to keep in touch with family and friends. They write notes when they are listening to their teachers and professors. They write papers for their teachers and professors, too. This book will help you when you have to write these papers. This kind of writing is called **academic writing**. It is different from other types of writing. It is more formal. It's also the style that teachers and professors expect from their students. Foreign language students *and* native speakers of English both have to learn how to write using the academic style.

INTRODUCTION: WRITING IN ENGLISH

Writing to communicate dates back thousands of years. Writing started as symbols on a cave wall, and then, about 3,500 years ago, the idea of an alphabet came up. Different languages use different writing systems.

Different languages also use different writing styles of organization. **English** organization, for example, is fairly simple. English uses a straight line from beginning to end. For instance, when English speakers read an article, they expect the article to have a beginning, a middle, and an end. The beginning should say what the article is going to be about, the middle should talk about the topic of the article, and the end should say what the article was about. Here is a diagram of the English style of writing.[1]

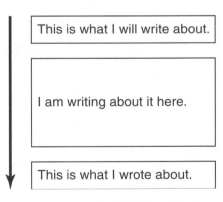

Diagram 1: English Organization

Other languages organize writing differently. For example, **Spanish** organization is similar to English, but the line from beginning to end isn't so straight. Spanish speakers write about the topic, but here and there they add something that is not directly related to the topic. To a Spanish speaker, this makes the writing more interesting.

(continued)

---

1 *Source*: Based on Kaplan, R.B. "Cultural thought patterns in intercultural education." *Language Learning*, 16 (1), 1966.

Here is a diagram of the Spanish style of writing.

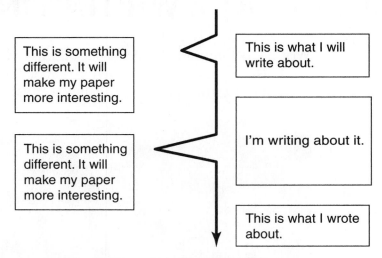

Diagram 2: Spanish Organization

The **Japanese** style of writing is often circular. This means that the topic comes at the end of the article. In fact, sometimes, the writer doesn't say what the topic is. Instead, the writer gives hints to help the reader guess the topic. Here is a diagram of the Japanese style of writing.

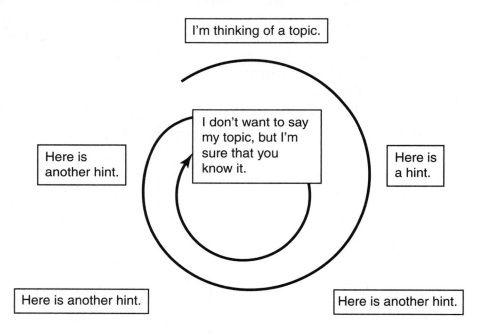

Diagram 3: Japanese Organization

It's important to understand that one style of writing isn't better than another, just as one language isn't better than another. The styles are just different. To be a successful writer in any language, you need to learn the writing style in addition to words and grammar rules.

In this book, you will learn the **American English** style of writing.

PART I

PARAGRAPH ORGANIZATION

CHAPTER 1: THE TOPIC SENTENCE

CHAPTER 2: SUPPORTING SENTENCES

CHAPTER 3: THE CONCLUDING SENTENCE

THE TOPIC SENTENCE

Predicting Personality

I VOCABULARY BUILDER

A. *With a partner, look at the definition of* personality. *Then, look at the list of words and circle the ones that could describe someone's personality. Don't use a dictionary. Your teacher will tell you the answers in a few minutes.*

personality /ˌpɚ·sə'næləti/ *n.* someone's character, especially the way he or she behaves towards other people

active	critical	outdoorsy
beautiful	energetic	outgoing
blond	fun-loving	patient
calm	hard-working	proud
creative	helpful	tall

What about you?

Which words would you use to describe your personality? Share your answers with a classmate. Say why.

One way you can predict (guess) someone's personality is to look at what that person is wearing. For example, what does a hat tell you about its owner? Look at the pictures. The first hat is a baseball cap. People who wear baseball caps are usually active, so you can predict that a person who wears a baseball cap is "active."

baseball cap

firefighter's hat

party hat

beret

fisher's hat

hard hat

B. *Complete these sentences about the hats above. Use words from the list on page 2 to describe the personality. Pay attention to the words in bold. They are verbs that people often use when talking about personality.*

1. Your hat **matches** your personality because it is a _____baseball cap_____, and you are _____active_____.

2. Your hat **goes with** your personality because it is a _____, and you are _____.

3. Your hat **says something** about your personality because it is a _____, and you are _____.

4. Your hat **corresponds to** your personality because it is a _____, and you are _____.

5. Your hat **matches** your personality because it is a _____, and you are _____.

6. Your hat **goes with** your personality because it is a _____, and you are _____.

Paragraph Organization in English

The basic unit of writing in English is a paragraph. A paragraph is usually short (about eight to fifteen sentences) and always includes a beginning, a middle, and an end.

The beginning is called the **topic sentence**. The middle part has **supporting sentences**. The end is called the **concluding sentence**. Look at this model paragraph. You can see each part of the paragraph in its own box. Now, read the paragraph.

Model Paragraph

Blood Types and Personality

TOPIC SENTENCE	Blood [1] types [2] may match certain personality traits [3].
SUPPORTING SENTENCES	The first blood type is Type O. People with this blood type are energetic. On the negative side, Type O people can often be too proud. The second blood type is Type A. Type A people are patient, but they can also be stubborn [4]. The third blood type is Type B. These people are creative but forgetful. The last blood type is AB. Type AB people are usually understanding of other people's feelings. However, they can also be critical of other people.
CONCLUDING SENTENCE	In short, certain personality characteristics go with a person's blood type.

[1] **blood** *n.* the red liquid in your body
[2] **type** *n.* a group of things that have similar qualities
[3] **trait** *n.* a quality
[4] **stubborn** *adj.* determined not to change

What about you?

In Japan, people say that blood types and personality are closely related. In the United States, astrological signs and personality are related. Is there a popular way of predicting someone's personality in your country? Tell a classmate about it.

The topic sentence in this paragraph tells the reader what the writer is going to talk about, the supporting sentences explain the writer's ideas, and the concluding sentence reminds the reader of the point the writer is making.

Identify the topic sentence, the supporting sentences, and the concluding sentence in this paragraph. Put a box around each part.

Colors and You

Your preference for a certain color says something about your personality. For example, if you like yellow, you are probably happy and outgoing. You're also very productive [1]. If your favorite color is blue, you are a calm person, happy with your life, and at peace with other people. If you prefer red, you are very active and love intense [2] experiences. If green is your color, you work on having a healthy body and a useful life. You also probably work to make society better. In conclusion, your favorite color says a lot about you.

[1] **productive** *adj.* doing many things	[2] **intense** *adj.* very strong

The Topic Sentence

In a paragraph, the first sentence is the **topic sentence**. The topic sentence is the main idea of that paragraph. It lets the reader know what the paragraph is going to be about. There are two parts to a topic sentence: the **topic** and the **controlling idea**. Look again at the topic sentence of the model paragraph.

> ➤ Blood types   may match certain personality traits.
>   topic   controlling idea

The topic is the subject that you're writing about. In this case, the subject is *blood types*. The controlling idea is what you are saying about a topic or the one part of the topic that you are writing about. The controlling idea limits the topic. In this case, the writer is writing about *personality traits* that correspond to blood types.

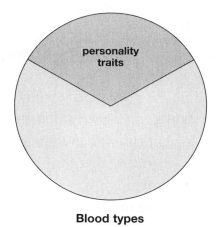

Blood types

However, instead of talking about personality traits, the writer could also write other paragraphs, about how blood types are used or about how you can learn your blood type. In those cases, the topic *blood types* is limited in other ways.

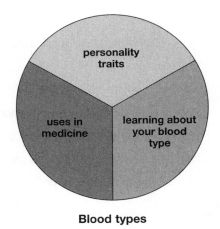

Blood types

Here is a topic sentence for a paragraph about *blood types* and the *uses in medicine*.

➤ Blood types   are very important to doctors.
    topic   controlling idea

Here is a topic sentence for a paragraph about *blood types* and *learning your blood type*.

➤ It's easy to learn your   blood type.
   controlling   topic

You can see in these examples that a topic can come **before** the controlling idea, or it can come **after** a controlling idea. It depends on how you want to write your topic sentence.

■ PRACTICE 2: **Identifying the Topic and Controlling Idea**

Circle the topic and underline the controlling idea in the following topic sentences.

1. (Twins) can have very different personalities.
2. It is possible (to be too nice).
3. Tom has a great personality.
4. Many people have problems with the winter blues.
5. Romantic people live longer lives.
6. It's surprising that reading palms can tell the future.
7. My brother is a very productive person.
8. There are many ways to learn about your personality.

a palm

More about Controlling Ideas

In addition to limiting the topic in a paragraph, the controlling idea usually adds a point of view to the topic sentence. The point of view is the **opinion** of the writer. This is because topic sentences that state facts don't encourage the reader to read the paragraph. A fact is true, but there's often not much more to say about it. Look at the following sentence.

> ➤ Elaine has a personality.

This isn't a good topic sentence because it states a fact. You can't argue with this statement, so the paragraph doesn't have much to say that is interesting.

If we add a **descriptive adjective**, however, the sentence becomes more interesting.

> ➤ Elaine has a **difficult** personality.

This is a good topic sentence because it stimulates the reader's interest. Now, the reader wants to find out why the writer thinks that Elaine's personality is difficult.

■ PRACTICE 3: **Identifying Topic Sentences**

Decide which of the following sentences work as topic sentences. If a sentence does, circle the topic and underline the controlling idea. If it doesn't, cross it out. Explain why.

1. ~~My mother was born into a large family.~~ *This is a fact.*
2. (My mother) was born into a happy family.
3. The professor gave a lecture.
4. The professor gave an exciting lecture.
5. Mark can sing like an opera star.
6. Mark can sing.
7. The house I grew up in was perfect for children.
8. The house I grew up in was sold.

As you can see, you can make a statement of fact into a topic sentence by adding a descriptive adjective. Another way to do this is to add *many* or *several* before a noun.

> ➤ Personality types   can be predicted in **many** ways.
>   topic   controlling idea

You could also add a **number** before the noun.

> ➤ Personality types   can be predicted in **four** ways.
>   topic   controlling idea

The paragraphs for these two topic sentences are going to talk about the different ways to predict personality types.

In the topic sentences below, circle the topic and underline the controlling idea.

1. (Hawaii) is a relaxing place to visit.
2. My dog has a perfect dog personality.
3. People go to college for many reasons.
4. My uncle Charlie is a crazy person.
5. There are four types of blood.
6. Yoshi is very energetic.
7. Many situations can cause sleeplessness.
8. There are three types of personalities.
9. Astrology deals with twelve signs.
10. Katy has a creative mind.

III STRUCTURE AND MECHANICS

Simple Sentences

In addition to being able to organize a paragraph, a good writer in any language needs to know the grammar of that language. Just as the paragraph is the basic unit of organization in English writing, the **sentence** is the basic unit of grammar. A sentence in English has at least a **subject** and a **verb**.

➤ People eat.
　 S　　　V

➤ We study.
　 S　 V

It's important to be able to recognize a sentence so that you can use the proper **punctuation**. All sentences in English begin with a capital letter and end with a period. The only exceptions are when you use a question mark (?) or an exclamation point (!) instead of a period.

Of course, the examples above are very short. Sentences that you write will probably be longer. The important lesson for a writer is to be able to see that a **complete sentence** has a subject and a verb. There may be words that follow the verb, but there is at least a subject and a verb.

➤ **People eat** meals three times a day.
　 S　　　V

➤ **We study** English in the morning.
　 S　 V

■ PRACTICE 5: **Identifying Sentences**

Some of the groups of words below make complete sentences. Some do not. Identify the complete sentences by putting a capital letter at the beginning and a period at the end. Cross out any groups of words that aren't complete sentences.

1.   A
     a good home is a good start for a baby.
2.   ~~ran away at twelve years of age~~
3.   too many difficulties at school
4.   some children are born with musical ability
5.   there many types of restaurants in my town
6.   i was eight years old
7.   is a beautiful backyard
8.   a little blue and lots of yellow
9.   the surroundings matched Joe's personality

Paragraph Format

Good paragraph format is important when you write in English. Here are six rules to remember:

1.   Put your name and date in the upper right-hand corner of the page.
2.   Always give your paragraph a title. Center the title above your paragraph.
3.   Indent the topic sentence of your paragraph (the first sentence). "Indent" means to leave about half an inch from the left margin before you start writing your first sentence. If you are typing, you can use the "tab" key.
4.   Start each sentence where the previous one ended. Do not go to a new line.
5.   Double space. This means to skip every other line.
6.   Stay inside the margins on the two sides of the paper.

Title

   It is easy to write a paragraph with good format. First, indent the first line of the paragraph about half an inch. Each sentence begins where the last sentence ended. Be sure that each sentence begins with a capital letter and ends with a period. Write on every other line. This is called double spacing. When your paragraph looks like this, you have a paragraph with good format.

Writing a Title

The **title** of a paragraph is the name of the paragraph. Titles are not usually complete sentences. They are one or more words that tell what the paragraph is about. You should capitalize the first and last word of your title. You should also capitalize other nouns, verbs, or adjectives in your title, but do not capitalize short words, such as prepositions and conjunctions (more about these later).

➤ **B**lood **T**ypes and **P**ersonality

➤ **C**olors and **Y**ou

■ PRACTICE 6: **Capitalizing Titles**

Add capital letters to these titles.

     R   *W*   *B*
1. red, white, and blue
2. six days in the small town of Pacifica
3. winter blues
4. a run through the forest
5. boys and girls
6. my vacation to Siberia
7. the joy of being alone
8. trying to determine a person's personality

The Writing Process, Part 1

Learning about writing, of course, leads to writing. However, it can be hard to know how to start writing. To help you, there are some steps you can follow. Together, these steps are called the **writing process**.

Step 1: Understanding the Assignment

In academic writing, the first step to the writing process is to be sure that you understand the assignment. To do this, you have to answer the following questions.

- What is the topic?
- How much should I write?
- When should I turn it in?
- What format should I use?
- Where do I get the information?

Step 2: Brainstorming

You have a broad topic (the assigned one). You may need to limit the topic. Then, you need to think about what you could say about that limited topic. You can do the following:

- Make lists.
- Write down ideas in any way on a piece of paper.
- Talk with a classmate.

Step 3: Organizing Your Ideas

Now look at all of your ideas and choose those that go together and that may form a paragraph. Remember that the first sentence in a paragraph is the topic sentence, and that a topic sentence needs a controlling idea to limit the topic. Once you have narrowed down your topic and grouped ideas that go together to support that topic, you are ready to write your topic sentence.

Your Turn

A. *Look at the topics below. Choose one of the topics. Go through the steps of the writing process. Then, write a topic sentence. The first one is done as an example.*

1. Food and personality
2. My blood type and personality
3. Colors and personality
4. Clothes and personality
5. Another idea about personality

Step 1: Understanding the Assignment

Topic: food and personality

Length: one short (5-7 sentences) paragraph

Due: tomorrow

Format: handwritten

Source of information: what I already know

Step 2: Brainstorming

◯	*food & personality — favorite food shows personality??*
	meat — strong, outgoing — like Josh
	vegetables — quiet, healthy — Sue
	chocolate — romantic — ME!

Step 3: Organizing Your Ideas

The brainstorming paper above has a list of foods and adjectives to describe people who like the food. There is also an example of a person for each food. This is a good start for organizing a paragraph. Now you can write your topic sentence.

➤  *Your favorite food says something about your personality.*

B. *After you have written your topic sentence, write three to five supporting sentences about your topic sentence. Then, write a concluding sentence to your paragraph. You will learn more about supporting sentences and concluding sentences in the next chapters of the book. Your main assignment now is to write a good topic sentence.*

Paragraph Checklist

Use this checklist when you are finished writing your paragraph. Check (✓) the box if your paragraph has the item.

> **1** My topic sentence is a sentence.
>
>   **a.** It has a subject and a verb. . . . . ❑
>   **b.** It starts with a capital letter and ends with a period. . . . .❑
>
> **2** My topic sentence has a clear topic. . . . .❑
>   Circle the topic.
>
> **3** My topic sentence has a clear controlling idea. . . . . ❑
>   Underline the controlling idea.
>
> **4** My paragraph has three parts. . . . . ❑
>   Put a box around the topic sentence, the supporting
>   sentences, and the concluding sentence.

Writing to Communicate . . . More

For more writing practice, go through the same process again with one of these topics. Then, write a paragraph.

1. Do you know another way of predicting personality? What is it?
2. What type of personality do you have?

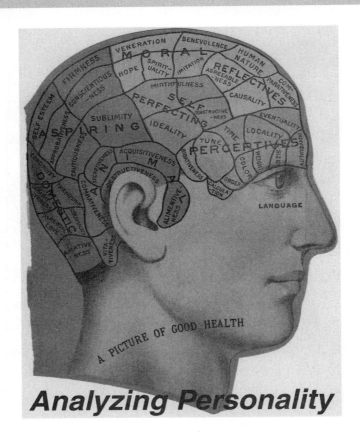

Analyzing Personality

I | VOCABULARY BUILDER

A. *Words that end in* **-ist**, **-yst**, *or* **-ian** *usually describe people. Look at these examples, and match each with its definition.*

___c___ **1.** an analyst

_____ **2.** an artist

_____ **3.** a guardian

_____ **4.** an idealist

_____ **5.** a psychologist

_____ **6.** a rationalist

a. someone who is legally responsible for someone else, especially a child

b. someone who bases their opinions and actions on intelligent thinking rather than on emotion

c. someone whose job it is to analyze or study something carefully

d. someone who is trained in psychology and studies people's minds

e. someone who produces art or who is a professional performer

f. someone who tries to live according to high standards or principles, especially in a way that is not practical

B. Read the sentences. Fill in the blank with the correct word from the box.

analyst	guardian	psychologist
artist	idealist	rationalist

1. Luke is very interested in how people's minds work. He loves talking to his friend who is a(n) _____*psychologist*_____.

2. Dana's job is to study the news carefully. Her job is a news _____.

3. When my sister became very sick, I became the _____ for her children. I took care of them.

4. Social workers are often _____ s. They want to help people because it is the right thing to do.

5. Michelangelo was a(n) _____. He painted the Sistine Chapel.

6. My father was a(n) _____. He used facts and examples to support his arguments.

II WRITING FOCUS

You learned in the last chapter that a paragraph is the basic unit of organization in English. A paragraph has three parts: the topic sentence, the supporting sentences, and the concluding sentence. The topic sentence consists of two parts: the topic and the controlling idea. In this chapter, you are going to learn about what makes the body of a paragraph: the **supporting sentences**.

What about you?

Have you ever heard of Sigmund Freud? If yes, share what you know with a classmate.

Supporting Sentences

The sentences that make up the body of your paragraph are called supporting sentences because they support the topic sentence. The model paragraph is about Sigmund Freud's description of the mind. Freud thought that there were three parts to the mind. In this paragraph, the supporting sentences talk about those three parts. Read the paragraph. Then, do Practice 1.

The Mind According to Freud

According to Freud, the mind has three parts. The biggest part is called the id. The id is the unconscious part of the mind and controls all the unconscious wants and needs. The superego is the second part. It comes from your experiences. It is your mother and father telling you what is right and wrong. The superego is part conscious and part unconscious. The last part is the ego. The ego is the conscious part of the mind. It deals with reality. In short, these three parts make up the Freudian mind.

Sigmund Freud, the father of modern psychology

■ PRACTICE 1: **Analyzing Model Paragraph 1**

1. Circle the topic of the topic sentence.
2. Underline the controlling idea.
3. How many supporting sentences are there? *(Remember NOT to include the concluding sentence.)*

Major Supporting Sentences

There are nine supporting sentences in this paragraph, but they are different in how they support the topic sentence. The first kind is called a **major** supporting sentence. These sentences support the topic sentence directly. In the model paragraph, there are three major supporting sentences.

➤ The biggest part is called the id.

➤ The superego is the second part.

➤ The last part is the ego.

Minor Supporting Sentences

The sentences that directly support the major supporting sentences are called **minor** supporting sentences. They are the explanations of the major supporting sentences, and they support the topic sentence indirectly.

Look at this diagram of Model Paragraph 1. It shows the paragraph sentence by sentence. Note the use of the following abbreviations:

TS = topic sentence
SS = major supporting sentence
ss = minor supporting sentence
CS = concluding sentence

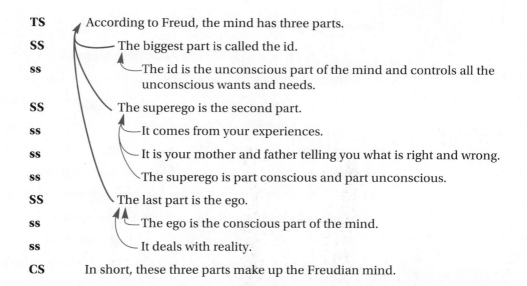

TS	According to Freud, the mind has three parts.
SS	The biggest part is called the id.
ss	The id is the unconscious part of the mind and controls all the unconscious wants and needs.
SS	The superego is the second part.
ss	It comes from your experiences.
ss	It is your mother and father telling you what is right and wrong.
ss	The superego is part conscious and part unconscious.
SS	The last part is the ego.
ss	The ego is the conscious part of the mind.
ss	It deals with reality.
CS	In short, these three parts make up the Freudian mind.

In this diagram, you can see how the body of a paragraph works. The **major** supporting sentences explain the topic sentence, and the **minor** supporting sentences explain the major supporting sentences. There is no "rule" about the number of minor supporting sentences. The first major supporting sentence only has one minor supporting sentence, the second has three minor supporting sentences, and the third has two minor supporting sentences. You as the writer make the decision about how many minor supporting sentences are needed.

■ PRACTICE 2: **Identifying Supporting Sentences**

Read Model Paragraph 2 on page 18. Analyze its organization by following these steps.

1. Put boxes around the three parts of the paragraph.
2. Circle the topic and underline the controlling idea in the topic sentence.
3. In the body of the paragraph, underline the **major** supporting sentences. How many are there?
4. Count the number of **minor** supporting sentences that support each of the major supporting sentences.

The Four Temperaments

Personality types can be grouped into four temperaments [1], according to some scientists. The first temperament is called the Artist. Artists are born for action. They are brave and outgoing, and they want to be the center of attention. Famous Artists include Picasso, Madonna, and Michael Jordan. The next temperament is the Guardian. People belonging to this group are the leaders of the world. They like order in their lives and in society. They lead families, schools, churches, hospitals, and governments. Queen Elizabeth is a Guardian, and so were George Washington and Mother Teresa. The third temperament type is called the Idealist. Idealists care deeply [2] about other people and want to help them. They believe that the best way for people to reach their goals [3] is to work together. Famous Idealists include Princess Diana and Mikhail Gorbachev. The last temperament is called the Rationalist. Rationalists want to understand how things work, how to do things, and especially how to build things. They want to learn all they can about science and technology. Marie Curie and Bill Gates belong to this group. In conclusion, people's personalities can be divided into these four temperaments.

[1] **temperament** *n.* the part of your character that makes you likely to be happy, angry, sad, etc.
[2] **deeply** *adv.* extremely or very much
[3] **goal** *n.* something that you hope to do in the future

What about you?

Can you think of other famous people who belong in each temperament? Share your answers with a classmate.

Now that you have read the model paragraph, look at the photos. What do the two people in each pair have in common?

Picasso

Madonna

George Washington

Mother Teresa

Mikhail Gorbachev

Princess Diana

Bill Gates

Marie Curie

Look at the diagram of this paragraph to check your answers to Practice 2 on page 17.

TS   Personality types can be grouped into four temperaments, according to some scientists.

SS   The **first** temperament is called the Artist.

ss   Artists are born for action.

ss   They are brave and outgoing, and they want to be the center of attention.

ss   Famous Artists include Picasso, Madonna, and Michael Jordan.

SS   The **next** temperament is the Guardian.

ss   People belonging to this group are the leaders of the world.

ss   They like order in their lives and in society.

ss   They lead families, schools, churches, hospitals, and governments.

ss   Queen Elizabeth is a Guardian, and so were George Washington and Mother Teresa.

SS   The **third** temperament type is called the Idealist.

ss   Idealists care deeply about other people and want to help them.

ss   They believe that the best way for people to reach their goals is to work together.

ss   Famous Idealists include Princess Diana and Mikhail Gorbachev.

SS   The **last** temperament is called the Rationalist.

ss   Rationalists want to understand how things work, how to do things, and especially how to build things.

ss   They want to learn all they can about science and technology.

ss   Marie Curie and Bill Gates belong to this group.

CS   In conclusion, people's personalities can be divided into these four temperaments.

Using Connectors with Major Supporting Sentences

Look back at the diagram of Model Paragraph 2. Notice the words in **bold** in the major supporting sentences. These words are called **connectors**. They connect ideas. The ones below are some of the most common.

Common Connectors	
first	next
second	last
third	

Connectors can be **adjectives**, as they are in the major supporting sentences in Model Paragraph 2.

➤ The **first** temperament is called the Artist.

➤ The **next** temperament is the Guardian.

➤ The **third** temperament type is called the Idealist.

➤ The **last** temperament is called the Rationalist.

Connectors can also be **transitions**. Look at these alternative ways of writing the major supporting sentences in Model Paragraph 2.

➤ **First**, there is the Artist temperament.

➤ **Next**, there is the Guardian temperament.

➤ **Third**, there is the Idealist temperament.

➤ **Last**, there is the Rationalist temperament.

Transitions come at the beginning of the sentences and are followed by a **comma**.

■ PRACTICE 3: **Using Transitions**

Here are five sentences about someone's morning activities. Indicate the correct order of the activities by filling in the blank with one of the words from the box above.

1. _____ , I eat breakfast.

2. _____ , I get dressed.

3. _____ , I leave for school.

4. _____ , I take a shower.

5. _____ , I wake up.

Parts of Speech

Most words in English fall into one of three parts of speech. These are **nouns**, **verbs**, and **adjectives**. Nouns are words for people, places, things, and ideas. Verbs are words for actions or states. Adjectives are words that describe nouns.

■ PRACTICE 4: **Identifying Nouns, Verbs, and Adjectives**

These are words from the exercise at the beginning of the chapter. Go to page 14 and review this exercise. Then, circle N if the word is a noun, V if the word is a verb, and A if the word is an adjective.

a.	analyst	Ⓝ V A		**f.**	idealist	N V A
b.	live	N V A		**g.**	mind	N V A
c.	study	N V A		**h.**	practical	N V A
d.	intelligent	N V A		**i.**	performer	N V A
e.	analyze	N V A		**j.**	produce	N V A

Lists and Commas

When you want to write a list, you need to remember three rules.

1. A list must have at least three items.
2. All the items in the list must be the same part of speech (nouns, verbs, or adjectives).
3. You must put a comma after each item except the last item in the list.

Look at these sentences.

➤ The **id**, the **ego**, and the **superego** make up the mind.
     N   N   N

➤ Scientists **think**, **experiment**, and **conclude**.
              V   V   V

➤ The primary colors are **red**, **blue**, and **yellow**.
                          A   A   A

For each sentence below, underline the items in the list. Identify the part of speech they are (nouns, verbs, or adjectives) and write it in the blank. Then, insert commas in the correct places.

adjectives   **1.** Chen is <u>polite</u>, <u>quiet</u>, and <u>practical</u>.

_____   **2.** In the morning, I get up shower and eat.

_____   **3.** When you go shopping, buy bananas oranges apples and grapes.

_____   **4.** Julie's new car is quiet smooth and comfortable.

_____   **5.** Hassan Kiyo Paulo and Ken are late today.

_____   **6.** The temperaments are Artist Guardian Idealist and Rationalist.

_____   **7.** A good basketball player can think run and jump fast.

_____   **8.** Carlos danced sang and acted in the movie.

IV WRITING TO COMMUNICATE

The Writing Process, Part 2

In the last chapter, you learned about the writing process and how it begins. It begins with three steps:

- Step 1: Understanding the assignment
- Step 2: Brainstorming
- Step 3: Organizing your ideas

When you organize, you narrow down your ideas (if necessary), and then write the topic sentence.

In this chapter, you will learn about the next step in the writing process: Step 4.

Step 4: Writing

In this step, you decide on the major points you need to support your topic sentence, and these ideas become your major supporting sentences. Then you decide which major supporting sentences need more detail. These details become your minor supporting sentences.

Your Turn

Here is your writing assignment for this chapter.

> Using the four temperaments and their descriptions in Model Paragraph 2, analyze your personality or the personality of someone you know.

A. Go through Steps 1–4 of the writing process. Follow the guidelines below.

Step 1: Understanding the Assignment

Your teacher tells you that you need to write one paragraph on this topic and turn it in tomorrow.

Step 2: Brainstorming

First, decide who you are going to write about. Yourself? A friend? A family member? Then, review the four temperaments and think about the person you have chosen. Write down the choice you make and give reasons for making this choice. You may want to start brainstorming by making a list.

best friend—Yuko	
Guardian because	
-always leading, makes decisions for us	
-likes order—in homework, in her room, in class	
-took care of father and brother in Japan	
-mom died when she was 8	
-had to have order	
-family is very important to her	
-wants to be the prime minister! She can lead the country!	

Step 3: Organizing Your Ideas

Writing the topic sentence will not be difficult for this paragraph. Your topic is the person you are analyzing, and the controlling idea is your decision about the temperament this person has.

➤ My best friend Yuko has a Guardian temperament.

Step 4: Writing

In the body of your paragraph, explain why you chose the temperament type. You might start like this:

My best friend Yuko has a Guardian temperament. First, Guardians are leaders, and Yuko likes to lead us around. We like that she makes decisions and plans for us. Second, . . .	

B. *After you have written your topic sentence and supporting sentences, write a concluding sentence to your paragraph. You will learn more about concluding sentences in the next chapter of the book.*

Paragraph Checklist

Use this checklist when you are finished writing your paragraph. Check (✓) the box if your paragraph has the item.

> **1** My topic sentence is a sentence.
> It has a subject and a verb. . . . .☐
>
> **2** My topic sentence has a clear topic. . . . .☐
> Circle the topic.
>
> **3** My topic sentence has a clear controlling idea. . . . .☐
> Underline the controlling idea.
>
> **4** The body of my paragraph has at least two major
> supporting sentences. . . . .☐
>
> **5** I have at least one minor supporting sentence for each
> major supporting sentence. . . . .☐
>
> **6** My paragraph has three parts. . . . .☐
>
> Put a box around the topic sentence, the supporting
> sentences, and the concluding sentence.

Writing to Communicate . . . More

For more writing practice, write a paragraph about someone you know. Choose one of the topics below.

1. Write about the personality type that this person has according to the four temperaments.

2. Write about his or her job, hobbies, or future plans. Here are some sample topic sentences.
   - My father has an interesting job.
   - My neighbor has a beautiful garden.
   - My friend Anna plans to have a wonderful future.

THE CONCLUDING SENTENCE

Family and Personality

I | VOCABULARY BUILDER

Look at the chart and the family tree. Then, identify the relationships between the people listed below. Work with a classmate.

Male	Female
husband	wife
father	mother
son	daughter
brother	sister
grandfather	grandmother
grandson	granddaughter
uncle	aunt
nephew	niece
father-in-law	mother-in-law
son-in-law	daughter-in-law
brother-in-law	sister-in-law
cousin	cousin

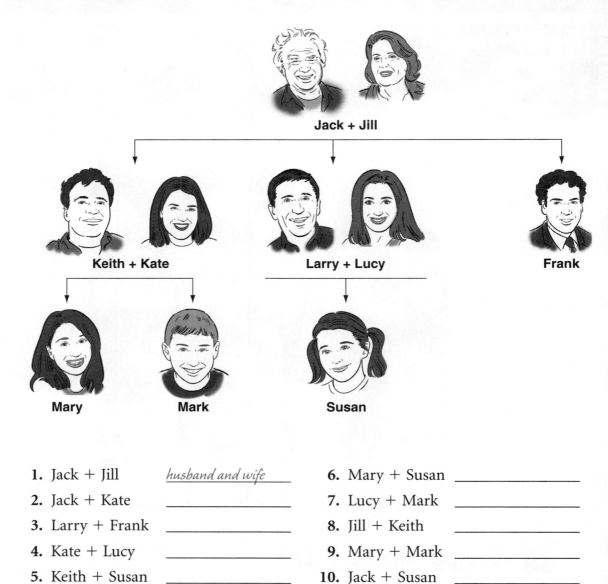

Jack + Jill

Keith + Kate   Larry + Lucy   Frank

Mary   Mark   Susan

1. Jack + Jill   *husband and wife*   6. Mary + Susan _____

2. Jack + Kate   _____   7. Lucy + Mark _____

3. Larry + Frank   _____   8. Jill + Keith _____

4. Kate + Lucy   _____   9. Mary + Mark _____

5. Keith + Susan   _____   10. Jack + Susan _____

II WRITING FOCUS

As you know, a paragraph has three parts: the topic sentence, the supporting sentences, and the concluding sentence. In this chapter, you are going to learn more about the **concluding sentence**.

The Concluding Sentence

The concluding sentence is the last sentence in a paragraph, so it should be an ending to the ideas in the paragraph. Read the model paragraph on page 27. Then, do Practice 1.

Model Paragraph

Birth Order

Birth order [1] may say something about the type of person you grow up to be. If you are the first child in your family, you are probably sure of yourself. You know that you can do things well. You also think you are a good leader, so you might be a little controlling [2]. If you are not the firstborn, you may have both older and younger brothers and sisters. This means that you probably get along well with people. You have many friends and are good in business. In fact, you may have your own business. Finally, if you are the baby of your family, you are the entertainer because you love to amuse [3] people. You may also be a little different because you don't want to be like your older brothers and sisters. In conclusion, your birth order can tell you about your personality.

[1] **birth order** *n.* the year you were born in relation to your brothers and sisters

[2] **controlling** *adj.* wanting people to do what you want them to do

[3] **amuse** *v.* to make someone laugh or smile

■ PRACTICE 1: **Analyzing the Model Paragraph**

1. Circle the topic of the topic sentence.
2. Underline the controlling idea.
3. Put a box around the concluding sentence. How does it compare to the topic sentence?

Types of Concluding Sentences

If you think that the concluding sentence in this model paragraph is almost like a topic sentence, you are right. This concluding sentence is a **restatement** of the topic sentence. It says the same thing as the topic sentence, but it uses different words. Another type of concluding sentence is a **summary** of the points in the paragraph. The writer summarizes, or briefly reviews, the major supporting sentences. Here is a summary concluding sentence for the model paragraph.

➤ In short, firstborn children are sure of themselves, middle-born children are social, and last-born children like to be different.

Transitions Used in Concluding Sentences

There's one more point about concluding sentences that you need to know. You should always signal the beginning of the concluding sentence. To do that, you can use the following transitions.

Transitions of Conclusion		
All in all, . . .	In conclusion, . . .	In short, . . .

Notice that these transitions are followed by a **comma**.

■ PRACTICE 2: **Choosing the Best Concluding Sentence**

Read this paragraph. Then, circle the letter of the best concluding sentence.

My Perfect Partner

My perfect partner must have three personality traits. First, he must have a good sense of humor. Life is often difficult. It's important to be able to laugh. Second, he must be kind. He must want to help people with his time and his money. Finally, he must love the outdoors. I spend a lot of time walking, hiking, and biking. I also love to camp and to sleep under the stars, so my perfect partner must love it, too.

a. All in all, partners must have the same personality traits.

b. In conclusion, my perfect partner must love to be outdoors.

c. In short, if someone wants to be with me, he must like to laugh, to help others, and to be outdoors.

■ PRACTICE 3: **Writing Concluding Sentences**

The following paragraph doesn't have a concluding sentence. Write two different ones for it. Be sure to use an appropriate transition.

Choosing a Dog

When you choose a dog as a pet, be sure to find one that matches your personality. For example, a poodle would be a good dog for you if you want your dog to learn a lot of tricks [1]. Poodles are very smart dogs. Next, if you like to stay in your house a lot, a Chihuahua might be a good dog for you.

poodle　　**Chihuahua**

Chihuahuas don't need a lot of exercise. If you have children, a pug is the dog for you. Pugs are gentle [2] and do not bite. Finally, if you want a good friend, you might choose a golden retriever. They will love you forever.

pug   golden retriever

---

[1] **trick** *n.* an action you teach a dog, like sitting or shaking hands

[2] **gentle** *adj.* kind and careful not to hurt anyone

1. A **restatement** concluding sentence:

   _____

   _____

2. A **summary** concluding sentence:

   _____

   _____

III STRUCTURE AND MECHANICS

Simple Sentences

You learned in Chapter 1 that a sentence must have a subject and a verb. A sentence with one subject-verb combination is called a **simple sentence**. It is also called an **independent clause**.

> I have two older brothers.
> S V
> Independent clause.

A simple sentence can have more than one subject or more than one verb.

> **Samira** and **I have** two older brothers.
> S   S V

> **They live** and **work** together.
> S   V   V

■ PRACTICE 4: **Identifying the Parts of a Simple Sentence**

For each sentence, circle the subject(s) and underline the verb(s). Write **S** *above each subject and* **V** *above each verb.*

$\overset{S}{}$ $\overset{S}{}$ $\overset{V}{}$

1. (José) and (Luis) <u>flew</u> to New York.

2. They stayed with their grandparents and visited many cousins.

3. Rosita is their oldest cousin.

4. She took them to many museums.

5. The boys loved New York and want to return soon.

6. Their grandparents and Rosita took them to the airport.

Compound Sentences

Not all sentences are simple sentences. Another type is the **compound sentence**. To make a compound sentence, you combine two independent clauses with a **coordinating conjunction** (**cc**). Here are the most common coordinating conjunctions.

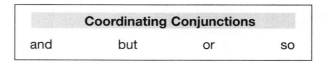

Coordinating Conjunctions			
and	but	or	so

➤ I have two older brothers, **and** she has two younger sisters.
   S V   cc   S   V
   Independent clause,   cc   independent clause.

➤ David is very quiet, **so** he needs a quiet dog.
   S   V   cc S V
   Independent clause,   cc independent clause.

Notice that you need to use a **comma** after the first independent clause.

■ PRACTICE 5: **Adding Commas**

Put a comma in the correct place in each sentence below.

1. Joe wants to have a dog, but his landlord won't let him.
2. Jin Soo was the oldest child in her family so she is a leader.
3. You like dogs and I like cats.
4. Jerry's dog likes to run every morning so Jerry gets lots of exercise.
5. We are friends but we don't like to do the same things.

■ PRACTICE 6: **Combining Sentences**

Combine the two simple sentences into one compound sentence. Use the correct coordinating conjunction (and, but, or, or so), *and add a comma in the correct place.*

1. I didn't have enough money for a plane ticket. I missed my sister's wedding.

   I didn't have enough money for a plane ticket, so I missed my sister's wedding.

2. Tomiko called her sister-in-law. She wasn't home.

   _____

3. Tomiko called her mother-in-law. They talked for thirty minutes.

   _____

4. I can move to my parents' house. I can get my own apartment.

   _____

5. My cousin and I live in different countries. We don't see each other often.

   _____

Combining Simple Sentences with the Same Subject

When you combine simple sentences with the same subject (with *and, but,* or *or*), it is possible to leave out the subject in the second sentence. When you leave out the subject in the second sentence, don't use a comma. The resulting sentence is a simple sentence with one subject and two verbs.

➤ Peter met Carol.   He fell in love immediately.
   S   V   S V
  Independent clause.   Independent clause.

➤ Peter met Carol **and** fell in love immediately.
   S   V   cc   V
  Independent clause.

■ PRACTICE 7: **Adding Commas in the Correct Places**

Put a comma in each sentence below if it is necessary.

1. We thought our dog would have three puppies, but she had five.
2. Kate's children always bring her flowers so her apartment smells wonderful.
3. Jack loves his new puppy and wants to get another.
4. I thought that my cousin was happy with his marriage so I was surprised when he moved out of his house.
5. My grandfather was born in Iowa but he grew up in Washington.
6. Angela works in the city and takes the train every day.

Combine the two sentences into one. Use a comma and the correct coordinating conjunction. If the two subjects are the same, don't use the second subject and don't use a comma.

1. Laura's uncle is a movie star. He lives in Hollywood.

   Laura's uncle is a movie star and lives in Hollywood.

2. Hiro and Yukiko got married last year. They had a baby last month.

   _____

3. Paula said she would come to class today. I don't see her.

   _____

4. Mike bought a pug for his daughter. She loves it.

   _____

5. Our grandfather was sick. We took him to the doctor.

   _____

6. My aunt loves animals. She has five cats.

   _____

IV WRITING TO COMMUNICATE

The Writing Process, Part 3

As you have learned, writing is a process and it has steps:
- Step 1: Understanding the assignment
- Step 2: Brainstorming
- Step 3: Organizing your ideas
- Step 4: Writing

Step 4: Writing

As you learned in the last chapter, Step 4 starts with writing the supporting sentences in your paragraph. Step 4 ends with writing a concluding sentence. Now that you know about the types of concluding sentences (a restatement of the topic sentence or a summary of the major supporting sentences), add that to this step. The result of this writing step is **the first draft** of your paragraph.

Before going on to the next step (rewriting) in the writing process, **take a break**. It will give you a "fresh eye" when you reread your paragraph.

Step 5: Rewriting

This step has two parts. The first part is called **revising.** When you revise your paragraph, look at the ideas, the organization, and the words. You might decide to add more information, or you might realize that you forgot to add a concluding sentence. Make these types of changes first.

The second part is called **editing**. When you edit your paper, look for grammar mistakes, word mistakes, and punctuation mistakes. These may be hard to find. You might ask a classmate to help you find them and correct them.

Step 6: Writing the Final Draft

You can go through Step 4 and Step 5 as many times as you want, but you will have to stop when the assignment is due. Then, write the paper that you will turn in to the teacher. This is called **the final draft**. Be sure to submit it in the format that the teacher requires (typed or handwritten).

Your Turn

In Part 1 of this book, you learned a lot about how to write a paragraph, and you learned a lot about the ways that people talk about personality. For your writing assignment, write a well-organized paragraph about one of the following topics.

1. What are the personality traits that your perfect partner must have?
2. You learned about some of the things that can be used to predict or analyze someone's personality: favorite hat, favorite color, blood type, birth order, and so on. Are there other things that can be used to know more about someone's personality? Write about one of them.

Paragraph Checklist

Use this checklist when you are finished writing the first draft of your paragraph. This checklist is part of the **rewriting** step in the process of writing. Check (✓) the box if your paragraph has the item.

1 My topic sentence is a sentence.
It has a subject and a verb. .... ❏

2 My topic sentence has a clear topic. .... ❏
Circle the topic.

3 My topic sentence has a clear controlling idea. .... ❏
Underline the controlling idea.

4 The body of my paragraph has major supporting
sentences and minor supporting sentences. .... ❏

5 My paragraph has a concluding sentence. .... ❏
It is a (*check one*)
a. restatement of the topic sentence. .... ❏
b. summary of the major supporting sentences. .... ❏

6 I used compound sentences with *and, or,
but,* or *so.* .... ❏

7 I used commas correctly in the compound
sentences. .... ❏

Writing to Communicate . . . More

For further writing practice, choose one of the topics below.

1. Does the kind of music someone likes say something about his or her personality? What does it say?

2. The word *stereotype* means "an idea of what a particular type of person is like, especially one which is wrong or unfair." People form stereotypes based on a person's culture or country. What is a common personality stereotype of people from your country?

I REVIEWING TERMS

Match the term on the left with its definition on the right.

_b_ **1.** a controlling idea

_____ **2.** a minor supporting sentence

_____ **3.** good paragraph format

_____ **4.** a topic sentence

_____ **5.** a topic

_____ **6.** a concluding sentence

_____ **7.** a major supporting sentence

_____ **8.** coordinating conjunctions

a. the subject that you're writing about

b. a word or words that limit your topic

c. a sentence that supports a major supporting sentence

d. when a paragraph has indentation, double spacing, margins, and a title

e. *and, but, so,* and *or*

f. the introduction to your paragraph

g. a sentence that directly supports the topic sentence

h. a restatement of your topic sentence

II REVIEWING IDEAS

Read this paragraph, and then follow the instructions on page 36.

Signs and Elements

There are four elements that go with the Western astrological signs. The first element is fire. People born in the fire signs are very active and a little pushy [1]. The second element is air. People who have an air sign think a lot and like to talk. Earth is the third element, and its people are practical and controlling. The last element is water. People with water signs are sensitive [2] and understanding. In short, these four elements add characteristics to the Western astrological signs.

---

[1] **pushy** *adj.* wanting to succeed so much that you are rude

[2] **sensitive** *adj.* able to understand other people's feelings

1. Circle the topic and underline the controlling idea in the topic sentence.
2. Diagram the paragraph on a separate piece of paper. See page 19 for a paragraph diagram.
3. What type of concluding sentence does this paragraph have? Circle one.

   a. restatement   **b.** summary

III ERROR ANALYSIS

*Five sentences have commas that are used correctly. Put **C** next to those sentences. The other three use commas incorrectly. Put **I** next to those sentences. Then, correct the mistakes by adding a comma or crossing one out. The first one is done for you.*

___C___ **1.** Chris is a psychology major, so he studies the theories of personality.

_____ **2.** Terri went to a doctor, a psychologist, an herbalist, and an astrologer.

_____ **3.** Kathy wants to buy a big car but her husband wants to buy a small car.

_____ **4.** Min Ho doesn't like to go to the dentist, but goes anyway.

_____ **5.** Aries Leo and Sagittarius are the three fire signs.

_____ **6.** Sara, Isabel, and Carla are sisters, but they have very different personalities.

_____ **7.** Helene likes chocolate so she drinks chocolate milk with lunch.

_____ **8.** My favorite cities in the United States are San Francisco, Seattle, and Chicago.

_____ **9.** There are fifteen students in my English class, and they come from fifteen countries.

_____ **10.** Eduardo lived in Canada for three years, and speaks English very well.

PART II
BASIC TYPES OF PARAGRAPHS

CHAPTER 4: DESCRIPTIVE PARAGRAPHS

CHAPTER 5: NARRATIVE PARAGRAPHS

CHAPTER 6: EXPOSITORY PARAGRAPHS

Describing People

I VOCABULARY BUILDER

When you describe someone's hair and face, you use certain words. Look at the words in the boxes below and at the diagram on the next page.

Adjectives			
black	brown	gray	straight
blond	curly	long	tan
blue	fair	short	white

Nouns		
bangs	freckles	scar
beard	moustache	wrinkles

Working with a classmate, fill in the two charts below with the words in the boxes on page 38. The number in each box indicates the number of words you can place in that box. You can use some words more than once.

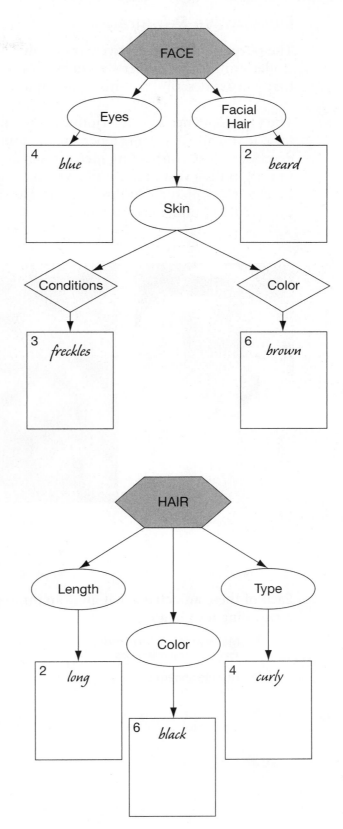

Descriptive Paragraphs

The purpose of a **descriptive paragraph** is to "paint" a picture in the reader's mind. The reader should be able to see the person, place, or object that you are describing in his or her mind.

The topic sentence in a descriptive paragraph has a topic and a controlling idea. If you are describing a person, the topic is the person you are describing. The **controlling idea** is often an **impression** of the person. An impression is a first thought that you have about something or someone. Look at these pictures of three people. Do you agree with the impressions that are listed under each picture?

Marwan	**Rodrigo**	**Akiko**
● worried	● angry	● shy
● wise	● proud	● calm

Each of these **adjectives** that gives an impression could be used as a controlling idea in a topic sentence.

➤ Marwan looks **worried**.
    topic   controlling idea

➤ Rodrigo seems **angry**.
    topic   controlling idea

➤ Akiko seems **shy**.
    topic   controlling idea

In a descriptive paragraph (as in all paragraphs), the supporting sentences must support the topic sentence. This means you should use words that support the impression in the controlling idea. Read Model Paragraph 1. As you read it, look back at the photo of Rodrigo and follow the description. Then, do Practice 1.

Model Paragraph 1

An Angry Man

Rodrigo seems angry in the photograph. On top of his head is a baseball hat turned backward. His forehead is smooth. Under his thick eyebrows, his dark eyes are looking straight into the camera. They are narrowed and unfriendly looking. His nose is straight and a bit flared [1]. His mouth is unsmiling, and his lips are turned down slightly. Below the mouth, the chin is pushed forward a bit, making him look even more unfriendly. All in all, when this picture was taken, it seems that Rodrigo wasn't in a very good mood.

[1] **flared** *adj.* wider at the bottom edge

■ PRACTICE 1: **Analyzing Model Paragraph 1**

1. What is the impression mentioned in the topic sentence?
2. How do the supporting sentences in the paragraph support this impression?
3. Underline the phrases that support the idea of Rodrigo being angry.

Prepositions of Place in Descriptive Paragraphs

In a descriptive paragraph, you want the reader to picture in his or her mind what is being described. To do this, you need to use **space order**. In other words, you describe a person from top to bottom, starting with the top of the head. (You will study more about space order in Chapter 8.)

Prepositions of place can help you with space order because they are words that relate two things in space. Can you find the prepositions of place in Model Paragraph 1? Circle them in the paragraph. If you're not sure, look at the list below.

Prepositions of Place				
above	behind	between	in front of	on
around	below	in	next to	under

Look at the picture. Complete each sentence with an appropriate preposition of place from the list on page 41.

1. A tall man is _____*in front of*_____ the line.

2. There is a short woman _____ him.

3. The woman has a hat _____ her head.

4. She also has a scarf _____ her neck.

5. She is _____ the tall man and the couple.

6. The couple is standing _____ each other.

7. There is a newspaper _____ this woman's big purse.

8. The last man in line is _____ an umbrella.

9. _____ the line, there is a sign with the name of the movie.

10. _____ the sign is the line of people.

The next model paragraph describes another person's hair and face. While you are reading, draw this person's portrait in the frame below. Use the prepositions of place to help you. After you read the paragraph, do Practice 1.

Model Paragraph 2

Jane Doe

Jane Doe is clearly an outdoorsy person. Her hair is short, blond, and curly. Her face is very tan, especially her forehead. Her eyebrows are very fair, and she has lots of small wrinkles around her large blue eyes. Her small straight nose is slightly peeling [1]. Her nose and cheeks are covered with freckles. She has two deep lines around her smiling mouth. Below her mouth, she has a small white scar going down to her chin. In short, this woman seems to enjoy being outdoors.

[1] **peeling** *adj.* when dead skin comes off

■ PRACTICE 3: **Analyzing Model Paragraph 2**

1. What is the topic of this paragraph? Circle it in the topic sentence.
2. What is the impression stated in the controlling idea? Underline it in the topic sentence.
3. Reread each supporting sentence carefully. Circle the words in each that support this impression. Look back at the Vocabulary Builder on page 38 for help with words you don't know.

Using Adjectives

Adjectives tell us about nouns. They usually come **before a noun**.

➤ Henry has a ***handsome*** face.

➤ The ***young*** girl played with her toys.

Adjectives can also come **after a linking verb**. Common linking verbs are *be, become, seem, look, feel, appear, taste, sound*.

➤ Henry's face **is *handsome***.

➤ The girl **seemed *young***.

➤ The sun **felt *warm***.

➤ The food **tastes *good***.

■ **PRACTICE 4: Using Linking Verbs and Adjectives**

Change the adjective phrases into sentences with linking verbs. Use the simple past form of the appropriate linking verb from the box.

appear	become	look	sound
be	feel	seem	taste

1. the long afternoon   *The afternoon seemed long.* _____

2. the delicious cake   _____

3. the loud music   _____

4. the soft kitten   _____

5. the beautiful baby   _____

6. the hot water   _____

7. the clean dishes   _____

8. the difficult test   _____

9. the fun party   _____

10. the empty room   _____

The Order of Adjectives before Nouns

When you describe a noun with two or more adjectives, you need to put the adjectives in the correct order. This chart shows the order and gives examples of adjectives for each type.

1 Opinion	2 Size	3 Age	4 Shape	5 Color	6 Origin	7 Material
beautiful	big	new	oval	blue	Californian	gold
handsome	small	young	round	green	French	rubber
pretty	long	old	square	red	Nepalese	silk
unattractive	short	elderly	straight	tan	Pakistani	wooden

➤ The **handsome young French** man gave us a smile.
      opinion   age   origin

➤ Linda's **long straight red** hair was below her waist.
      size   shape   color

➤ My grandmother is a **small elderly Chinese** woman.
      size   age   origin

➤ He gave her a **beautiful green silk** scarf.
      opinion   color   material

■ PRACTICE 5: Putting Adjectives in the Correct Order

Complete the sentences with the adjectives in parentheses. Make sure you use them in the correct order. You do not need to use commas here.

1. Rita's daughter always has a _____*cute big red*_____ bow in her hair.
    (big / cute / red)

2. The _____ hat looks great on you.
    (silk / yellow / pretty)

3. His _____ glasses rest on his _____
    (brown / unattractive)   (red / big)
nose.

4. The _____ man looked happy to see his
    (Southern / elderly)

_____ car.
    (big / pink / old)

5. The _____ earrings looked beautiful.
    (Native American / round / blue)

Your Turn

For this writing assignment, use one of the photos below.

Write a paragraph that describes the hair and face of the person in the photo. Follow this procedure.

1. For the topic in your topic sentence, use "John Doe" or "Jane Doe."
2. For the controlling idea, use a one- or two-word impression of this person.
3. Write your supporting sentences using good space order. Include words that will support your impression. Look back at the chart on page 39 for vocabulary.
4. Write a concluding sentence that restates your topic sentence.
5. Switch paragraphs with one of your classmates. Try to guess the person that your classmate wrote about while he or she tries to guess the person you wrote about. Your teacher may also want to do this as a class activity.

If you need help with the writing process, go to Appendix 1: *Going Through the Writing Process* on page 122.

Paragraph Checklist

Use this checklist when you are finished writing your paragraph. This checklist is part of the **rewriting** step in the process of writing. If you like, you can switch paragraphs with your classmate and check each other's paragraph.

1. My topic sentence has a clear topic. . . . . ❑
2. The controlling idea in my topic sentence is an impression. . . . . ❑
3. My paragraph uses space order. . . . . ❑
4. I used phrases in the body of my paragraph that support my impression. . . . . ❑
5. I used prepositions of place correctly. . . . . ❑
6. I used adjectives in the correct order. ❑

Writing to Communicate . . . More

For more writing practice of descriptive paragraphs, choose one of these topics.

1. Describe the hair and face of a friend or family member.
2. Look in a mirror and describe yourself.
3. Describe your perfect boyfriend or girlfriend.

CHAPTER 5

NARRATIVE PARAGRAPHS

Telling Stories

I VOCABULARY BUILDER

When you tell a story, you usually use the past tense. Therefore, it's important to know the past tense of verbs.

Review the simple past of irregular verbs by working with a classmate and filling out the chart below.

Verb	Simple Past	Verb	Simple Past
drink	*drank*	pay	
drive		put	
fall		ride	
feel		sleep	
fly		speak	
get		steal	
give		tell	
leave		wake up	

Narrative Paragraphs

One way to support your topic sentence is to tell a story. When you tell a story in your paragraph, you are writing a **narrative paragraph**. A narrative paragraph tells a story about something that happened in the past. This type of paragraph has the same three parts as other paragraphs: a topic sentence, a body of supporting sentences, and a concluding sentence.

Read this model paragraph. Then, do Practice 1.

Model Paragraph

A South American Adventure

an active volcano

My trip to Chile was quite memorable [1]. First, I flew to Santiago, the capital, but I didn't stay there long. Second, I went to Valparaíso on the coast. Valparaíso is built on hills, and it has wonderful old funiculars [2] that climb up the the hills. At the top, the view over the ocean is fantastic. After that, I drove with a friend to Pucón in the Lake District. Pucón is built at the foot of an active volcano. At night, we could see red hot rocks exploding from the top of the volcano into the dark sky. It was fantastic! Next, we went to the island of Chiloé. Chiloé is best known for its many old wooden churches, and my friend wanted to see one in Tenaún, a village far from the coast. We drove slowly for hours over dirt roads until we finally reached the village. I took her picture in front of the church, and we had lunch at a local restaurant. Finally, I returned to Santiago to fly home. I was sad to leave Chile, but I have my memories of this wonderful trip.

[1] **memorable** *adj.* very good or unusual, and worth remembering

[2] **funicular** *n.* a small railway that goes up the side of a hill or mountain

What about you?

Tell a classmate about a memorable trip that you took.

■ PRACTICE 1: **Analyzing the Model Paragraph**

1. Put boxes around the three parts of the paragraph: the topic sentence, the body, and the concluding sentence.
2. Circle the topic and underline the controlling idea.
3. What type of concluding sentence ends this paragraph, a restatement or a summary?
4. How many supporting sentences are there?

Transitions in Narrative Paragraphs

In a narrative paragraph, you tell a story of events in the order that they happened. In other words, you order your sentences based on **time order**. (You will study more about time order in Chapter 8.) Using **transitions of time order** can help the reader follow the story. Here are some common transitions of time order.

Transitions of Time Order	
First, . . .	Next, . . .
At first, . . .	Then, . . .
Second, . . .	After that, . . .
Third, . . .	Finally, . . .

Notice that all of these transitions go at the beginning of a sentence and are followed by a **comma**.

■ PRACTICE 2: Finding Time Order Transitions

Look again at the model paragraph on page 49. Put a box around the time order transitions.

III STRUCTURE AND MECHANICS

Complex Sentences

In Chapter 3, you learned about simple sentences and compound sentences. There is a third type of sentence: the **complex sentence**. A complex sentence combines an independent clause and a dependent clause. Look at this sentence.

> ➤ Michael arrived   after Kim left for the airport.
> Independent clause   dependent clause.

A **dependent clause** has a subject and a verb, but it isn't a complete sentence. It cannot stand alone; it must be connected to an independent clause. Look at this sentence.

> ➤ After she hung up the phone, Rita fixed dinner.
> Dependent clause,   independent clause.

Notice that there is a **comma** after the dependent clause. This sentence can also be written with the dependent clause after the independent clause without changing the meaning. When this happens, there is no comma.

> ➤ Rita fixed dinner   after she hung up the phone.
> Independent clause   dependent clause.

The dependent clause in the sentences on page 50 begins with *after*. *After* is an example of a **subordinating conjunction**. All dependent clauses of **time** begin with a subordinating conjunction. There are many subordinating conjunctions. Here are some common ones for narrative paragraphs.

Subordinating Conjunctions				
after	before	until	when	while

Look at the following sentences. Notice that the dependent clause can come before or after the independent clause.

➤ **Until** the train arrives, we can't go anywhere.

➤ We can't go anywhere **until** the train arrives.

■ PRACTICE 3: Inserting Commas

Insert commas in the correct place in the sentences below if it is necessary.

1. I couldn't speak English before I went to the United States.
2. Please don't call me until you read my e-mail.
3. While Sam was on vacation an earthquake damaged his home.
4. Lucia always reads the newspaper when she eats breakfast.
5. After they retired my parents went on a lot of trips.
6. Before Michael left Japan he visited Nara.

Verb Tenses with Dependent Clauses of Time

When you write a sentence with a dependent clause of time, pay attention to the verb tenses in the dependent clause and in the independent clause. Here are two rules.

1. If you write about **future time**, use the simple present in the dependent clause and the future in the independent clause.

➤ **When** we **arrive** in Alaska, we**'ll buy** some warm clothes.
      simple present   future

➤ I**'m going to take** a walk **before** the sun **sets**.
      future   simple present

2. If you use *while* to begin the dependent clause, use the present progressive or past progressive in that clause.

➤ **While** you**'re taking** photographs, I**'ll go** to the museum.
            present progressive

➤ Jack **watched** television **while** Maria **was getting** dressed.
                                          past progressive

■ PRACTICE 4: **Using Correct Tenses with Dependent Clauses of Time**

Complete the paragraph with the correct form of the verbs in parentheses.

Sam's Vacation

While his wife _____*is traveling*_____ to faraway places with her friends,
(1. travel)
Sam will do some work on their house. First, after he _____on a
(2. decide)
color, he _____the bathroom. While he _____in
(3. paint)   (4. work)
the bathroom, he _____the shower. Next, he will clean up the
(5. fix)
yard. Before he _____that, he _____to the store
(6. do)   (7. go)
to get some fertilizer. After that, Sam will build the new desk that his wife wants.
After he _____the desk, he _____done with his
(8. finish)   (9. be)
home improvements. When his wife _____, she will certainly be
(10. return)
surprised to see the results of Sam's work.

■ PRACTICE 5: **Writing Complex Sentences**

*Combine the two sentences. Make one a dependent clause, using the
subordinating conjunction in parentheses. Use a comma if necessary and use
the correct tenses.*

1. Jim took a taxi to the airport. He flew to India.

   (before) *Jim took a taxi to the airport before he flew to India.* OR _____

   Before Jim flew to India, he took a taxi to the airport.

2. Annie won't travel by boat. She gets some medicine for her stomach.

   (until) _____

3. Ling will travel to Canada. Her mother will take care of her children.

   (when) _____

4. Harry was taking a shower. Kate tried to call him.

   (while) _____

5. The sun came up. Toshi went running.

   (when) _____

6. Jack traveled to Bangkok. He came home with lots of souvenirs.

   (after) _____

7. There won't be fireworks. The sun goes down.

   (until) _____

8. We will spend nine hours on the train. We will arrive in Chicago.

   (before) _____

Your Turn

Before you write a narrative paragraph, it's a good idea to brainstorm and answer these basic questions.

- Where did this story take place?
- Who are the people in the story?
- What happened?
- When did it happen?
- Why did it happen?
- How did the story end?

For your writing assignment, choose one of these topics.

1. Write about a trip that you took. It can be a long trip or a weekend getaway. You can write about how good it was or about how bad it was.

2. Each of the pictures below suggests a story. Brainstorm on your own or with a classmate about each picture. Who is the main person in the picture? How did he or she get there? What happens next? Be creative! There is no right or wrong answer.

3. This is a series of pictures that tell a story. Brainstorm about it on your own or with a classmate. Who are these people? What is going on in their lives? Be creative! There is no right or wrong answer.

Now that you have your topic and brainstormed about it, write a narrative paragraph based on it. Remember the steps of the **writing process**. See the flowchart below.

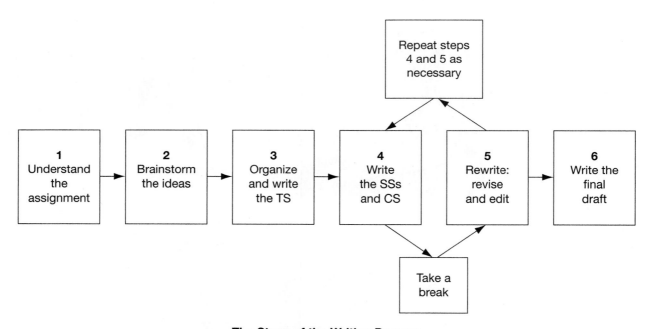

The Steps of the Writing Process

If you need more help, go to Appendix 1: *Going Through the Writing Process* on page 122.

Paragraph Checklist

Use this checklist when you are finished writing your paragraph. This checklist is part of the **rewriting** step in the process of writing. If you like, you can switch paragraphs with your classmate and check each other's paragraph.

1 I have a topic in the topic sentence. . . . .❑

2 I have a controlling idea in the topic sentence. . . . .❑

3 The story in the body of my paragraph supports
the topic sentence. . . . .❑

4 I have a concluding sentence in my paragraph. . . . .❑

5 I have _____ transitions of time in my paragraph.
(*Write the number.*)

6 There are _____ sentences with dependent clauses of time
in my paragraph. (*Write the number.*)

7 I used commas correctly with dependent clauses. . . . .❑

Writing to Communicate . . . More

For more writing practice, choose one of these topics.

1. Write about an event in your life. This could be a dangerous event, a happy one, a funny thing that happened, or any other story you want to tell.

2. Write about a famous person from your country. Briefly tell the story of his or her life.

3. Write a story for children.

EXPOSITORY PARAGRAPHS

Communicating

I   VOCABULARY BUILDER

Below are ten verbs for communicating. Some are for speaking, and some are for writing. Some can be for both. With a classmate, write each verb in the correct column.

communicate	say	talk
discuss	shout	text-message
e-mail	speak	write
phone		

Speaking	Writing
communicate	*communicate*
say	*e-mail*

Expository Paragraphs

In an **expository paragraph**, you explain something. There are many ways of explaining something. One way is to explain your ideas by **giving examples**. Read this model expository paragraph. Then, do Practice 1.

Model Paragraph

Ancient [1] Systems of Communication

Many ancient cultures had interesting ways of communicating long-distance. For example, the Incas in South America used *quipus* to send messages from one village to another. Quipus were ropes that had a series of knots [2] tied into them. The color and number of knots gave information or told a story. Second, smoke signals were used by the Chinese and Native North Americans. They sent simple messages by covering and uncovering fires slowly and quickly. As a final example, native people in West Africa used drums to carry messages across distances. The strength and tone [3] of the beat delivered different messages. In conclusion, in ancient times, there were different ways of sending messages to people far away.

a *quipu*

What about you?
Do you know any other ways that ancient people communicated? Tell a classmate.

■ **PRACTICE 1: Analyzing the Model Paragraph**

1. Circle the topic and underline the controlling idea.
2. How many major supporting sentences are there in this paragraph?
3. What are the transitions that begin each major supporting sentence? Put a box around them.
4. What is explained in this paragraph? How is it explained?

Transitions in Expository Paragraphs

Most expository paragraphs use **logical order** to order the major supporting sentences. In other words, the writer organizes ideas based on what he or she thinks is logical. The writer of the model paragraph above thought that it was logical to use this order: quipus, smoke signals, and drums. Another writer might use a different order. (You will learn more about logical ordering in Chapter 8.) When you explain something by **giving examples**, you use transitions of example and of logical order.

Transitions of Logical Order		
First, . . .	Second, . . .	Next, . . .
First of all, . . .	Third, . . .	Finally, . . .

Transitions of Example	
For example, . . .	For instance, . . .
As a [first, second, final] example, . . .	

Notice that all of these transitions go at the beginning of a sentence and are followed by a **comma**.

III STRUCTURE AND MECHANICS

Using Transitions

Up to now, you have seen transitions of time order, logical order, example, and conclusion. There are many other transitions. Look at this chart that lists some common ones according to their meaning.

Time Order	Logical Order	Example	Addition	Contrast	Result	Conclusion
first	first	for example	also	however	therefore	all in all
at first	first of all	for instance	in addition			in conclusion
second	second	as a [first, second, final] example	moreover			in short
third	third					
next	next					
then	finally					
after that						
finally						

You have seen how transitions connect ideas between the major parts of a paragraph. Transitions can also **connect two sentences** that follow each other. Look at the way the transitions are used in the following sentences.

➤ There are many ways to contact me. **For example,** you can write me, call me at home, call me on my cell, e-mail me, or text-message me.

➤ I e-mailed Paul about the meeting. **In addition,** I called him.

➤ Granny has a phone in her house. **However,** she refuses to get a cell phone.

➤ The electricity wasn't working. **Therefore,** we couldn't watch the news.

There are three points to notice:

1. You must use a capital letter.
2. After each transition, you need to put a comma.
3. The first word after the transition does not start with a capital letter unless it is a name.

■ PRACTICE 2: **Using Transitions**

Connect the two sentences in each item. Use the transition in parentheses. Be sure you use commas and capital letters correctly.

1. Alexander Graham Bell invented the telephone. He invented

   the phonograph.

   (then)   *Alexander Graham Bell invented the telephone. Then, he invented the*

   phonograph.

2. I read two newspapers every day. I watch the news on TV.

   (in addition)   _____

3. Be sure to turn off the lights. Lock the door.

   (after that)   _____

4. I left a message for Ed. He hasn't called me back.

   (however)   _____

5. Katrina got an MP3 player for her birthday. She can download music.

   (therefore)   _____

■ PRACTICE 3: **Using Appropriate Transitions**

Fill in each blank with the correct transition. Choose one of the transitions in the chart on page 58. Use commas and capital letters correctly.

1. Min's old computer stopped working. _____*Therefore*_____, he had to buy a new one.

2. Joe wanted to go to the party. _____ he couldn't go because he had to work late.

3. Before you buy a computer, you should read about them.

   _____ you should ask your friends about their computers.

4. I hate to make phone calls to people I don't know. _____ I don't mind writing them a letter or an e-mail.

5. I like many kinds of music. _____ I like rock and roll, classical, and folk music.

6. We got home at 2:00 A.M. and got up at 6:00 A.M. _____ we didn't get a lot of sleep.

(continued)

7. First, Emily reads the newspaper every morning. _____ she reads blogs online.

8. First, we're going to China. _____ we'll go to Vietnam.

9. Many animals have ways of communicating with each other. _____ honeybees tell other bees where to find food by dancing.

10. Hans writes books about global warming. _____ he gives lectures about it.

■ PRACTICE 4: **Writing Sentences**

Add a sentence after each transition. Be sure that it relates well to the sentence before the transition.

1. My friend called to say she couldn't go to the movies with me.

   Therefore, _____

2. Gabriella was certain that her cell phone was the best.

   However, _____

3. I called a lot of people today. In addition, _____

   _____

4. I called a lot of people today. For example, _____

   _____

5. First, you have to buy all the ingredients for the cake. Then, _____

   _____

IV WRITING TO COMMUNICATE

Your Turn

With a classmate, discuss examples of the topics listed in the chart on page 61. Write your ideas in the chart. Then, choose the topic that most interests you and write a paragraph. Start by writing a topic sentence. Remember to add a controlling idea to your topic. At the end, write a concluding sentence. For additional help with the writing process, go to Appendix 1: *Going Through the Writing Process* on page 122.

Examples of Body Language	Uses of a Cell Phone	Ways of Learning Vocabulary in a Second Language

Paragraph Checklist

Use this checklist when you are finished writing your paragraph. This checklist is part of the **rewriting** step in the process of writing. If you like, you can switch paragraphs with your classmate and check each other's paragraph.

1. My topic sentence has a clear controlling idea. . . . . ☐

2. I used _____ examples to support my topic sentence. *(Write the number.)*

3. My paragraph has a concluding sentence. . . . . ☐

4. I used _____ transitions in my paragraph. *(Write the number.)*

5. I used commas and capital letters appropriately with these transitions. . . . . ☐

Writing to Communicate . . . More

For more writing practice, choose one of the following topics and write a paragraph about it. Remember to narrow your topic down to one appropriate for a paragraph.

1. How we communicate
2. How we communicated in the past
3. How we will communicate in the future

I REVIEWING TERMS

A. *Match the sentence to the type of paragraph it is talking about.*

_____ **1.** This paragraph explains something.

a. descriptive

_____ **2.** This paragraph tells a story.

b. narrative

_____ **3.** This paragraph paints a picture for readers.

c. expository

B. *Identify the parts of the sentence. Put the number in front of the term.*

```
         3                          4
   ┌─────────────┐          ┌──────────────┐
➤  When Carla went to college,  she had a terrible time.
   └─────────────┘          └──────────────┘
          1                          2
```

—— adjective   —— independent clause

—— dependent clause   —— subordinating conjunction

II REVIEWING IDEAS

*Read each paragraph below. Then, circle **N** if it is a narrative paragraph, **D** if it is a descriptive paragraph, or **E** if it is an expository paragraph.*

Paragraph 1   **N   D   E**

> **To Marry or Not to Marry**
>
> There are many benefits of getting married. For example, married people live longer than single people. It's better for your emotions to be married, and happier emotions help you have a healthier body. Another benefit is that you have someone to share the household work with. It's hard to do everything by yourself. Another example is that when you are married, you have someone to enjoy experiences with. In summary, these benefits show that being married is better than being single.

The Danger of Driving

I had a scary experience driving home from work last week. I was driving on Market Street in rush-hour traffic, and I could see that the driver of the car in front of me was talking on his cell phone. One of his hands was holding his phone, and the other was holding the steering wheel [1]. I could see that the traffic light [2] in front of him was turning red, but he didn't see it. As he drove through the intersection [3], a truck hit his car on the passenger side. Luckily, no one was seriously injured in this accident, but both the car and the truck were badly damaged. In short, even though I wasn't directly involved in the accident, it was still frightening.

[1] **steering wheel** *n.* a wheel that you turn to control the direction of a car

[2] **traffic light** *n.*

[3] **intersection** *n.* the place where two streets meet

III ERROR ANALYSIS

*Five sentences have correct punctuation. Put **C** next to those sentences. The other five use commas incorrectly. Put **I** next to those sentences. Then, correct the mistakes by adding a comma or crossing one out. The first two are done for you.*

<u> C </u> **1.** We took a long slow trip across the country before we moved to the West Coast.

<u> I </u> **2.** In addition, we took a side trip, to Mexico.

_____ **3.** My friend hates the cool weather. Therefore, he preferred our drive through the southwestern part of the United States.

_____ **4.** The restaurant served only organic food.

_____ **5.** After you finish your homework you can help me with the dishes.

_____ **6.** After that we can go to the movies if you want to.

_____ **7.** I grew up on a huge corn farm.

_____ **8.** The weather has been very dry. Therefore my beautiful green lawn has turned brown.

_____ **9.** Until we get our phone connected we can't call anyone.

_____ **10.** The phone company said that someone would come yesterday. However, no one came.

CHAPTER 7: UNITY

CHAPTER 8: COHERENCE

CHAPTER 9: COHESION

UNITY

Experiencing Emotions

I   VOCABULARY BUILDER

The pictures below are called "emoticons" or "smileys." They were originally invented to show emotion, or feeling, by using ordinary printed characters in written communication. For example, a smiley face showing happiness was written like this **:)** and an unhappy one like this **:(**. Later, software was developed to make actual smiley faces: ☺ ☹.

Match each emoticon to the correct emotion. Then, with a partner, discuss situations in which you feel these emotions. Fill in the chart on page 67.

| 1 | 2 | 3 | 4 | 5 |

6

7

8

9

10

Emotion	Emoticon	Situations
anger	1	*When someone steps on my foot and doesn't say sorry.*
boredom		
embarrassment		
fear		
joy		
love		
pride		
sadness		
surprise		
worry		

What about you?

When did you feel one of these emotions strongly? Tell your classmate the story.

II WRITING FOCUS

Unity

In the Introduction, on pages xv–xvi, you learned that different languages have different organizational patterns. The organizational pattern in English is a straight line from beginning to end. This means that a paragraph in English is about one topic, which is limited by the controlling idea. Every sentence in the paragraph must relate to that topic and controlling idea.

Read the model paragraph on page 68. Then, do Practice 1.

Model Paragraph

Basic Emotions

Some scientists think that there are six basic emotions. The first is love. Love comes in many forms, such as love for your husband or wife, your children, or your friends. Second, there is joy. Feelings of joy can go from simple happiness because you are satisfied with your life to feeling ecstatic because you won the lottery. The third emotion is surprise. When something happens that you didn't expect, you feel surprised. For example, if your friends give you a birthday party and don't tell you, you will be surprised when you walk in the door. Next, there is anger. Anger includes being annoyed because your pen won't work and being jealous because your friend is flirting [1] with someone else. I got jealous last week when my girlfriend danced with José. The next emotion is sadness. Sadness happens when you are disappointed in something or when you are depressed about something. Finally, there is the emotion of fear. Your fear can go from being nervous because you didn't study for a test to being scared because something threatens [2] your life. In short, these six types of emotions are in all of us.

feeling ecstatic

What about you?

What emotion is the strongest? Share your thoughts with a classmate.

[1] **flirt** *v.* to behave toward someone as though you are sexually attracted to him or her, but not in a very serious way

[2] **threaten** *v.* to be likely to harm or destroy something or someone

■ PRACTICE 1: **Analyzing the Model Paragraph**

1. What type of paragraph is this? Circle one.
   descriptive   narrative   expository
2. What is the topic of this paragraph? Circle it in the topic sentence.
3. What is the controlling idea? Underline it in the topic sentence.
4. How many major supporting sentences are there?
5. Do all the major supporting sentences support the topic sentence? Why or why not?
6. Do all of the minor supporting sentences support their major supporting sentence? Why or why not?

The answer to the last question is the key to understanding the concept of **unity**. Unity means that all the sentences support the topic sentence in a paragraph. In the sample paragraph, the topic is "emotions" and the controlling idea is "six basic." The sentence *I got jealous last week when my girlfriend danced with José* does not help to explain what anger is, so it doesn't belong in this paragraph. It should be crossed out.

A supporting sentence that does not belong to a paragraph is called an **irrelevant sentence**. This type of sentence has no relation to the topic sentence because it doesn't support it. As you learned, English writing is a "straight line" from the beginning of a paragraph to the end of a paragraph.

■ PRACTICE 2: **Finding Irrelevant Sentences**

Read these paragraphs. Each paragraph has one irrelevant sentence. Cross it out and be prepared to say why the sentence is irrelevant.

1.
                         An Unhappy Boy

It was clear that George was an unhappy little boy. His eyes were wet with tears. His nose was red, and he was breathing heavily. His mother also looked unhappy. His lips were tightly closed. They were turned down, and his lower lip was stuck out. He sat in the corner with his arms folded across his chest. All in all, he looked very unhappy.

2.
                    Eyebrows and Emotions

Eyebrows alone can sometimes show a person's emotional state. If your friend's eyebrows are high up, he or she is probably surprised. If the eyebrows are closed together in a frown, your friend may be angry. Eyebrows that are straight say that your friend is happy and content. If the eyebrows are lowered a little, it could mean that your friend is scared. Very lowered eyebrows can mean that your friend is very sad. In this case, you should probably offer to take him or her out for a cup of coffee or tea. In short, the next time you see a friend, look at the eyebrows to see how he or she feels.

3. **Reasons to Cry**

People cry in many different situations to express many different emotions. The most common situation is when people get physically hurt, but people cry also because of sad events in their lives. When people experience loss, such as someone dying or breaking up with them, they often show their sadness by crying. People also cry at very happy times in their lives. At weddings, especially, you'll see a lot of people crying because they are happy. Seeing a newborn baby, winning a race, or watching a happy movie can also bring tears to the eyes. My brother never cries at movies, though. Another situation in which people cry is when they are very angry or very scared. These emotions are so strong that people cry even if they don't want to. In short, crying can happen at many different times and can express many different things.

III STRUCTURE AND MECHANICS

Combining Sentences

You have learned a lot of ways to make your writing better, such as using good organization and having unity. Another way to make your writing better is to use different kinds of sentences. You have already learned how to combine sentences in many ways, using different **connectors** (transitions, coordinating conjunctions, or subordinating conjunctions). In fact, you have learned how to combine the same two sentences in four different ways! Look at these examples.

➤ The directions confused Jack. Jill explained them.
   Independent clause.   Independent clause.

1. Using a transition:

   ➤ The directions confused Jack. **However,** Jill explained them.
      Independent clause.   T,   independent clause.

2. Using a coordinating conjunction:

   ➤ The directions confused Jack, **but** Jill explained them.
      Independent clause,   cc   independent clause.

3. Using a subordinating conjunction (dependent clause second):

   ➤ The directions confused Jack **until** Jill explained them.
      Independent clause   sc   dependent clause.

4. Using a subordinating conjunction (dependent clause first):

   ➤ **Until** Jill explained them, the directions confused Jack.
      Sc   dependent clause,   independent clause.

Combine the two sentences in each item. Use the connectors in parentheses. Be sure to use capital letters, commas, and periods correctly.

1. Sam graduated from college. He is very happy.

   (so) _____ *Sam graduated from college, so he is very happy.* _____

   (therefore) _____

2. Tim is very boring. Tina loves him.

   (but) _____

   (however) _____

3. You get embarrassed. Your face turns red.

   (and) _____

   (then) _____

   (after) _____

4. Chang was bored watching TV. He turned it off.

   (therefore) _____

   (so) _____

5. Pierre was cooking dinner. His wife was reading a book.

   (and) _____

   (while) _____

6. John and Elizabeth fell in love. They got married.

   (and) _____

   (next) _____

   (before) _____

IV WRITING TO COMMUNICATE

Your Turn

Refer to the facial expressions on the emoticons on pages 66 and 67 to do this assignment. Choose one of the types of paragraphs and topics listed on page 72. Make sure that your paragraph has unity and that you don't use irrelevant sentences. If you need help with the writing process, go to Appendix 1: *Going Through the Writing Process* on page 122.

1. **Descriptive**

   Describe the facial expression on one of the emoticons or on one of your friends.

2. **Narrative**

   Choose one of the emotions shown on the emoticons' faces. Write a story about an event in your life when you experienced the emotion.

3. **Expository**

   Choose one of the emoticons and write about examples of situations when someone might feel this emotion.

Paragraph Checklist

Use this checklist when you are finished writing your paragraph. If you like, you can switch paragraphs with your classmate and check each other's paragraph.

1 The type of paragraph I wrote is (check one)

    a. descriptive. . . . .❏

    b. narrative. . . . .❏

    c. expository. . . . .❏

2 My topic sentence has a clear topic and controlling idea. . . . . . .❏

3 My paragraph has a concluding sentence. . . . .❏

4 My paragraph has unity. In other words, there are no irrelevant sentences in my paragraph. . . . .❏

5 I used the following connectors correctly (check all that you used):

    a. transitions . . . .❏

    b. coordinating conjunctions . . . .❏

    c. subordinating conjunctions . . . .❏

Writing to Communicate . . . More

For more writing practice, choose one of these topics to write about.

1. What does your best friend's face look like when he or she is happy? Describe it.

2. What was the happiest day of your life? Write a story about it.

3. Choose a common event in someone's life (getting married, having a baby, graduating from school, etc.). Give examples of emotions that you might feel on that day.

Learning about Family History

I VOCABULARY BUILDER

A. *Look at the picture with a classmate. What do you see? What do you think is happening?*

B. Now take turns reading the story below out loud to each other. Fill in each blank with the correct preposition.

Delivering Mail in 1860

Pony Express riders carried mail_____ St. Joseph, Missouri,
(1. from/to)

_____ San Francisco, California, _____ 1860 and
(2. from/to)   (3. between/to)

1861. _____ one trip, a rider changed horses many times
(4. During/To)

because the horses got tired. _____ the horses, the riders got
(5. For/Like)

tired, too, but they couldn't rest _____ the last stop.
(6. until/through)

This is a picture _____ a rider _____
(7. for/of)   (8. in/on)

Chadron, Nebraska. This ride took place _____ June 20
(9. at/on)

_____ 1860 _____ about 10:00 A.M. You can
(10. in/on)   (11. at/on)

see the Pony Express rider going _____ town
(12. by/through)

_____ his horse. _____ him, there is a cowboy
(13. above/on)   (14. at/in front of)

_____ saddle bags. The mail is _____ the bags.
(15. in/with)   (16. inside/on)

People loved to watch the Pony Express riders and looked _____
(17. beyond/out of)

their windows and _____ their chairs every time the riders
(18. by/from)

came _____ town.
(19. by/into)

II WRITING FOCUS

Coherence

In the last chapter, you learned about unity, which is one characteristic of good writing. Another characteristic of good writing is **coherence**. If your paragraph has good coherence, the supporting sentences are in **good order**. "Good order" depends on the type of paragraph you are writing.

Descriptive Paragraphs and Space Order

For descriptive paragraphs, good coherence is based on **space order**. A descriptive paragraph should draw a picture of the object so that the reader can see the object in his or her mind. To do this successfully, you need to describe an object in **space** because that's how people are used to seeing objects. For example, if you describe a person, start at the top and go down. Similarly, when you describe a place, start from one place (usually the door) and describe from left to right or from right to left. Read this model descriptive paragraph. Then, do Practice 1.

Model Paragraph 1

Austin's Lunch Counter

My grandfather's restaurant, or lunch counter [1], was very simple. When you entered through the front door, to your right, you could see a counter. Behind the counter was all the equipment needed to serve food: an oven, a stove, a big refrigerator, and a shelf with lots of dishes and pans. In front of the counter, you could see ten red stools [2]. Behind the stools were ten or twelve tables lined up in two rows. The tables were all the same size, and they all had four red chairs around them. In short, Grandpa Austin's lunch counter was very plain [3] in its appearance.

[1] **counter** *n*. the place where you are served in a restaurant

[2] **stool** *n*. a tall chair with no back or arms

[3] **plain** *adj*. simple; without decoration

■ PRACTICE 1: **Analyzing Model Paragraph 1**

1. Put boxes around the three parts of the paragraph.
2. Circle the topic and underline the controlling idea.
3. Where does the writer start the paragraph? What direction does the writer take—left to right or right to left?
4. What prepositions are used to show where something is? (*Hint*: There are seven prepositions of place.)
5. Can you picture in your mind what this lunch counter looked like? Draw a picture of it. How does the use of space order help you?

You probably were able to draw a picture of Austin's lunch counter without too much difficulty because the writer used space order to describe the parts of the restaurant.

Narrative Paragraphs and Time Order

For narrative paragraphs, good coherence is based on **time order**; that is, the order of the supporting sentences is based on **time**. Read this model narrative paragraph. Then, do Practice 2.

Model Paragraph 2

Surviving the Quake

My grandmother often told us about her sad story of survival [1] during the 1906 earthquake in San Francisco. Like many San Franciscans, she was asleep in her bed when the earthquake happened. At first, she didn't know what was happening. Then, she fell out of bed. After that, she tried to reach her parents' bedroom, but she couldn't because the ground shook [2] for so long. After the quake was over, she and her family ran out of their apartment. They didn't want to be inside the apartment if an aftershock [3] occurred. After they were outside for a few hours, her father left and went downtown to check on his restaurant, but he never came back. The family searched for him, but he was never found. In short, this was the saddest story my grandmother ever told.

---

[1] **survival** *n.* the continuation of life after a dangerous situation

[2] **shook** *v.* the past tense of **shake**; to move quickly from side to side and up and down

[3] **aftershock** *n.* a small earthquake, usually one in a series that happens after a larger earthquake

■ PRACTICE 2: **Analyzing Model Paragraph 2**

1. Put boxes around the three parts of the paragraph.
2. Circle the topic and underline the controlling idea.
3. What connectors are used to show time order? (*Hint*: There are three transitions and two subordinating conjunctions.)
4. How does the use of time order help you understand the paragraph?

The answer to the last question is that a narrative paragraph is a story, and the events of a story are told in the order that they happened. You can't mix up the order because the reader will become confused.

Expository Paragraphs and Logical Order

Coherence for most expository paragraphs is different. In these types of paragraphs, you use **logical order**. Logical order is based on **logic**, or the way people think or reason. The ideas of time and space are very similar for everyone, but the idea of logic is not. That is why the order of supporting sentences in expository paragraphs can change. "Logic" to one writer may or may not be logical to another writer. Read this model expository paragraph. Then, do Practice 3.

Model Paragraph 3

<table>
<tr><td>

Learning about the Past

I never met my great-grandfathers, but I've learned a lot about one of them from several sources. First of all, many facts of his life came from official records. I know that he was born in 1888 in Nebraska and that he died in 1929 from diabetes [1]. I also know where he lived during his lifetime because I looked in census [2] records. Second, family members told me stories about him. For example, I know that he liked to cook and sometimes wouldn't let my great-grandmother in the kitchen. Finally, I have two artifacts [3] that tell me about him. One artifact, a painting, tells me that he enjoyed nature but wasn't very good at painting it. The other artifact, a letter to his wife, tells me that he loved my great-grandmother very much. In conclusion, I never actually met my great-grandfather, but I feel that I know him a little.

</td></tr>
</table>

[1] **diabetes** *n.* the disease of having too much sugar in your blood

[2] **census** *n.* a counting of the population

[3] **artifact** *n.* an object from the past

> **What about you?**
>
> What do you know about your grandparents or your great-grandparents? Discuss your answer with a classmate.

1. Put boxes around the three parts of the paragraph.
2. Circle the topic and underline the controlling idea.
3. Diagram this paragraph on a separate piece of paper.
4. What transitions introduce the major supporting sentences?

If you diagrammed this paragraph correctly, you know that there are three major supporting sentences:

➤ First of all, many facts of his life came from official records.

➤ Second, family members told me stories about him.

➤ Finally, I have two artifacts that tell me about him.

Remember that the coherence of an expository paragraph depends on logic. The writer of this paragraph thought that it was logical to discuss official records first, family stories second, and artifacts third. However, that's not the only correct order. Here are some other possibilities:

- family stories, artifacts, official records
- artifacts, official records, family stories
- official records, artifacts, family stories

The order of sentences, or coherence, of an expository paragraph depends on the writer.

■ PRACTICE 4: **Rewriting the Model Paragraph**

*Rewrite Model Paragraph 3. Use a different order of supporting sentences. You can use the same transitions—**first of all**, **second**, **finally**—or you can use other transitions.*

Coherence and Connectors

Coherence depends on the type of paragraph you are writing and on the order this paragraph uses.

- **Descriptive paragraphs** use **space order**. The order cannot change once a direction has been started.
- **Narrative paragraphs** use **time order**. The order cannot change.
- Most **expository paragraphs** use **logical order**. The order depends on what the writer thinks is logical or what makes sense.

Using **connectors** helps you order your sentences so that your paragraph will have good coherence. Refer to the following chart for appropriate connectors to use with each kind of order. For a more complete chart, see Appendix 2: *Common Connectors* on page 124.

CONNECTORS

	Transitions	Subordinating Conjunctions	Prepositions	Adjectives
Space Order			to your right to your left above [something] around behind below between [two things] in in front of next to on under	
Time Order	first at first second third next then after that at last in the end finally	after before until when while		the first [thing] the second the third the next the last the final
Logical Order	first first of all second third next last last of all finally			the first [thing] the second the third the next the last the final

III STRUCTURE AND MECHANICS

Avoiding Fragments

In Chapter 1, you learned that a sentence, or independent clause, must have a subject and a verb. If a group of words is missing one of these parts, it becomes a **fragment**. It is not a complete sentence. The fragment may have a capital letter and a period, but it is still incorrect. Look at the following fragments. (✗ = *incorrect*)

✗ Met her at the family party last night. (The subject is missing.)
   V

✗ Anna very good mother. (The verb is missing.)
   S

✗ Uncle Joe taking a lot of pictures. (The helping verb is missing.)
   S   -ing form

Another type of fragment happens when a dependent clause stands by itself and is not linked to an independent clause.

    X   When Grandma turned eighty-five.

    X   Before she left for the airport.

These dependent clauses need to be attached to an independent clause to become correct.

    ➤   **When Grandma turned eighty-five**, we had a big party.
         Dependent clause,   independent clause.

    ➤   We didn't decide **before she left for the airport.**
         Independent clause   dependent clause.

■ PRACTICE 5: **Identifying Fragments**

*Decide if each item below is a sentence or a fragment. Write **S** if it is a sentence and **F** if it is a fragment. If it is a fragment, explain why.*

   S   **1.** My grandmother came to the United States in 1951.

   F   **2.** That the best restaurant in town. *The verb is missing.*

  _____ **3.** While we were visiting our parents.

  _____ **4.** Saw Kim in the hospital.

  _____ **5.** Almost 100 relatives attended the family reunion.

  _____ **6.** Wanted Ed to accompany me downtown, but he was busy.

  _____ **7.** My two favorite kinds of restaurants Thai and Mexican.

  _____ **8.** Many of my relatives live in Brazil.

  _____ **9.** Grandfather cooking the holiday dinner.

  _____ **10.** The scientist studied the old artifacts.

IV WRITING TO COMMUNICATE

Your Turn

Form a small group of classmates. Discuss these questions. Take notes as you talk. For question 1, try to draw the object as your classmate describes it.

1. Do you have an artifact from your family's history? This could be a piece of jewelry or a piece of furniture that used to belong to your grandparents or great-grandparents.

2. Did anyone in your family experience a disaster, such as an earthquake, a fire, a flood, or a tsunami?

3. What lessons did you learn from your grandparents or great-grandparents? Are these lessons useful?

After your group discusses the questions, choose one topic and write a paragraph about it. If you need help with the writing process, go to Appendix 1: *Going Through the Writing Process* on page 122.

Paragraph Checklist

Use this checklist when you are finished writing your paragraph. If you like, you can switch paragraphs with your classmate and check each other's paragraph.

1 My topic sentence states my opinion. . . . .❏

2 My paragraph is a(n) (*check one*)
   a. descriptive paragraph. . . . .❏
   b. narrative paragraph. . . . .❏
   c. expository paragraph. . . . .❏

3 I used (*check one*)
   a. space order. . . . .❏
   b. time order. . . . .❏
   c. logical order. . . . .❏

4 I used _____ connectors. (*Write the number.*)

5 My paragraph doesn't have any fragments. . . . .❏

Writing to Communicate . . . More

For more writing practice, choose one of these topics to write about.

1. Write a description of someone's house or a room in the house.
2. Pick a year before you were born and write about a typical day in that year for your parents, grandparents, or great-grandparents.
3. What occupations did your grandparents have? That is, how did they earn a living?

Dating and Marrying

I VOCABULARY BUILDER

A. *Below are pairs of verb phrases that describe dating and marriage customs in many Western countries. For each pair, indicate which one has to happen first.*

1. __2__ go out on a date
   __1__ ask someone out

2. _____ get engaged
   _____ get married

3. _____ ask someone out
   _____ get turned down

4. _____ fall in love
   _____ date for a while

5. _____ break up
   _____ date for a while

6. _____ get married
   _____ fall in love

7. _____ get engaged
   _____ date for a while

8. _____ get divorced
   _____ get married

B. *Write sentences to complete these two stories. Use verb phrases from Exercise A on page 82.*

Story 1

1. Jaime asked Anne out.

2. _____

3. _____

4. _____

5. Jaime and Anne broke up.

Story 2

1. _____

2. Daniel and Laura dated for a while.

3. _____

4. _____

5. _____

II WRITING FOCUS

Cohesion

Cohesion is another characteristic of good writing. If your paragraph has good cohesion, the sentences in your paragraph "stick together." That is, there are connections that relate them to each other. Good cohesion helps your reader because your paragraph is easier to read. For example, read this paragraph. It does not have good cohesion, so it is difficult to read.

Sample Paragraph 1

Fairy Tales and Love

In fairy tales [1], true love always wins. In a fairy tale *Sleeping Beauty,* an evil witch [2] causes a beautiful princess to fall into a deep sleep. A beautiful princess must stay asleep until a handsome prince finds a beautiful princess and kisses a beautiful princess. A handsome prince finds a beautiful princess and wakes a beautiful princess up with a kiss. A beautiful princess and a handsome prince live happily ever after. A story shows that love is always possible.

[1] **fairy tale** *n.* a story for children in which magical things happen

[2] **witch** *n.* a woman who has magic powers, especially to do bad things

To make this paragraph better, you need to add connections between the sentences. There are several kinds of connections, or **cohesive devices**.

Connectors

Connectors are one kind of cohesive device. You learned in previous chapters that connectors can be transitions, coordinate conjunctions, subordinate conjunctions, prepositions, and adjectives. For a more complete list of connectors, see Appendix 2: *Common Connectors* on page 124. Adding connectors to Sample Paragraph 1 improves the cohesion, so the paragraph is easier to read.

Sample Paragraph 2

Fairy Tales and Love

In fairy tales, true love always wins. **For example,** in a fairy tale *Sleeping Beauty*, an evil witch causes a beautiful princess to fall into a deep sleep. A beautiful princess must stay asleep until a handsome prince finds a beautiful princess and kisses a beautiful princess. **At last,** a handsome prince finds a beautiful princess and wakes a beautiful princess up with a kiss. **In the end,** a beautiful princess and a handsome prince live happily every after. **In short,** a story shows that love is always possible.

The Definite Article

Another cohesive device is the **definite article** (*the*). Use the definite article the second time you mention an item. Look at the following example.

➤ Tim brought <u>an apple</u> to his teacher. <u>**The** apple</u> was a gift.

The definite article in the second sentence connects these two sentences.

Here's the sample paragraph again. It now uses definite articles to make connections between the sentences.

Sample Paragraph 3

Fairy Tales and Love

In fairy tales, true love always wins. For example, in **the** fairy tale *Sleeping Beauty*, an evil witch causes a beautiful princess to fall into a deep sleep. **The** beautiful princess must stay asleep until a handsome prince finds **the** beautiful princess and kisses **the** beautiful princess. At last, a handsome prince finds **the** beautiful princess and wakes **the** beautiful princess up with a kiss. In the end, **the** beautiful princess and **the** handsome prince live happily ever after. In short, a story shows that love is always possible.

Personal Pronouns

Another cohesive device is **personal pronouns**. For a chart showing the personal pronouns, look on page 87. The following examples show how pronouns can connect sentences.

➤ Greg read a fairy tale to his **daughter. She** loved the story.

The personal pronoun (*she*) in the second sentence connects these two sentences.

➤ The **story** was about a frog and a princess. In **it**, the frog turned into a handsome prince.

Here, the personal pronoun (*it*) connects the two sentences.

Demonstrative Pronouns

The final cohesive devices are demonstrative pronouns. See page 88 for a chart showing the demonstrative pronouns. The following examples show how sentences can be connected using these devices.

➤ **Some fairy tales** have lessons. **These** teach children right from wrong.

The demonstrative pronoun (*these*) in the second sentence connects these two sentences.

➤ The frog story has **a lesson. This** lesson is about beauty.

The demonstrative adjective (*this*) connects these two sentences.

Here is the original paragraph again. This version has all the pronouns and other cohesive devices it needs to make it easy to read and understand.

Model Paragraph 1

Fairy Tales and Love

In fairy tales, true love always wins. For example, in the fairy tale *Sleeping Beauty*, an evil witch causes a beautiful princess to fall into a deep sleep. The beautiful princess must stay asleep until a handsome prince finds **her** and kisses **her**. At last, a handsome prince finds the beautiful princess and wakes **her** up with a kiss. In the end, **they** live happily ever after. In short, **this** story shows that love is always possible.

What about you?

Did your parents tell you fairy tales when you were a child? Tell one to a classmate.

Look at the following paragraph. Circle all the cohesive devices (3 connectors, 16 personal pronouns, 2 definite articles). Then, draw arrows to show the connections for the pronouns and the definite articles. If you need to review personal pronouns, look at the chart on page 87.

What about you?

How did people find a marriage partner 100 years ago in your country? Tell a classmate.

Dating and Marriage

One hundred years ago in the United States, dating before marriage had to be done in a certain way. First, if a man wanted to go out with a woman, he had to ask permission[1] from her father. Then, he could only see her if her sister or her friend went out with them. He could never be alone with her until after they were engaged. If the man wanted to marry the woman, he had to ask her father before he could ask her. Sometimes couples were in love when they got married, but sometimes they weren't. A marriage was like a business agreement. In short, the process of dating in the early 1900s was very strict [2].

[1] **permission** *n.* the act of allowing someone to do something

[2] **strict** *adj.* demanding that everyone follows the rules

III STRUCTURE AND MECHANICS

Being Consistent with Person and Number

One of the most important cohesive devices is a **pronoun**. Pronouns are used when you want to refer back to a noun that came earlier in your paragraph. The noun is called an **antecedent**. Look at this example.

➤ Mick bought a **diamond ring** for **Mary**. **She** loves **it**.
           antecedent   antecedent pronoun pronoun

She is the pronoun that refers to *Mary*, and *it* is the pronoun that refers to *a diamond ring*. By using the pronouns, we know that the two sentences are connected.

Personal Pronouns and Adjectives

As discussed on page 85, there are many types of personal pronouns in English. This chart lists them.

PERSONAL PRONOUNS

	Singular				Plural			
	Subject	Object	Possessive		Subject	Object	Possessive	
			adjective	pronoun			adjective	pronoun
first person	I	me	my	mine	we	us	our	ours
second person	you	you	your	yours	you	you	your	yours
third person	he she it	him her it	his her its	his hers	they	them	their	theirs

When you are writing a paragraph, be consistent when you use these pronouns and their antecedents. You need to be consistent with "person" and "number." Look at these sentences.

Third-person plural:

➤ **Parents** give **their children** cell phones.

Then, **they** can keep in touch with **them**.

Third-person singular:

➤ **A parent** can give a cell phone to **his child**.

Then, **he** can keep in touch with **her**.

Second-person singular and third-person singular:

➤ **You** can give a cell phone to **your child**.

Then, **you** can keep in touch with **her**.

You can see that in each sentence, the pronouns refer back to a noun that is the same in terms of person and number.

■ PRACTICE 2: **Correcting Errors in Person and Number**

This paragraph has nine mistakes in pronoun usage. Correct the underlined pronouns by changing the person or the number.

Parents are better able to keep in touch with their children now that there are cell phones. Twenty years ago, when parents had a son, for example, <u>you</u> often didn't know where <u>she</u> had gone. If <u>your</u> son were late coming home, <u>you</u> couldn't do anything except wait for <u>them</u>. Now, parents can simply call <u>your</u> child, or the child can call <u>him</u>. In short, <u>I</u> am glad that <u>your</u> children have cell phones.

Demonstrative Pronouns

Like personal pronouns, demonstrative pronouns must agree in number with their antecedent. This chart shows the four demonstrative pronouns in English. Look at the sentences below. Note that a demonstrative pronoun can stand alone or be used as an adjective before a noun.

DEMONSTRATIVE PRONOUNS

		Singular	Plural
Meaning	**Close**	this	these
	Far	that	those

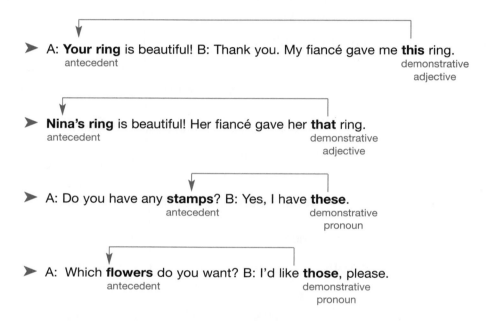

➤ A: **Your ring** is beautiful! B: Thank you. My fiancé gave me **this** ring.
   antecedent   demonstrative adjective

➤ **Nina's ring** is beautiful! Her fiancé gave her **that** ring.
   antecedent   demonstrative adjective

➤ A: Do you have any **stamps**? B: Yes, I have **these**.
                        antecedent   demonstrative pronoun

➤ A: Which **flowers** do you want? B: I'd like **those**, please.
               antecedent   demonstrative pronoun

■ PRACTICE 3: **Using Demonstrative Pronouns**

Fill in each blank below with a demonstrative pronoun. Use each pronoun— **this, that, these, those**—*only once.*

My Broken Heart

My heart was broken in a quick five minutes yesterday. My friend and I went to a restaurant for lunch. After we sat down, I noticed a handsome man sitting across the room at another table. I said to my friend, "Look at _____ man over there. Isn't he handsome?"
1.

My friend said, "He's OK."

"Just OK? He's beautiful!" I said. "_____ eyes! I'm in love!"
2.

Then, the man got up and started walking toward our table. I was so nervous. He smiled at us, looked at the chair, and asked, "Can I use _____ chair? My girlfriend is meeting us and we need another
3.
chair."

My friend said, "Sure, take it." I was crushed! Then, she looked at me and said, "_____ things happen."
4.

IV WRITING TO COMMUNICATE

Your Turn

1. With a classmate, brainstorm examples to support each of the following topics. Write your ideas in this chart.

Ways to Ask Someone Out	Places to Go on a Date	Ways to Break Up with Someone

2. Pick one of the topics above to write a paragraph. Your topic sentence will be

   There are many _____.

3. Write your paragraph. If you need help with the writing process, go to Appendix 1: *Going Through the Writing Process* on page 122.

Paragraph Checklist

Use this checklist when you are finished writing your paragraph. If you like, you can switch paragraphs with your classmate and check each other's paragraph.

> **1** My paragraph has a topic sentence and a controlling idea. . . . . . ☐
>
> **2** I used these cohesive devices in my paragraph *(check all that apply)*:
>   **a.** transitions . . . . ☐
>   **b.** definite articles . . . . ☐
>   **c.** personal pronouns . . . . ☐
>   **d.** demonstrative pronouns . . . . ☐
>
> **3** All the pronouns in my paragraph agree in number and person with their antecedent . . . . ☐

Writing to Communicate . . . More

For more writing practice, choose one of these topics.

1. Happy couples
2. Famous divorces
3. Ways to live happily ever after

I REVIEWING TERMS

*If the statement is true, circle **a** and if the statement is false, circle **b**.*

1. The ordering of supporting sentences according to time is called space order.

   a. true   **b.** false

2. Your paragraph has unity if it has no irrelevant sentences.

   a. true   **b.** false

3. Ordering of supporting sentences according to logic is called time order.

   a. true   **b.** false

4. An expository paragraph describes something physically.

   a. true   **b.** false

5. The order of supporting sentences in a narrative paragraph cannot change.

   a. true   **b.** false

6. If you correctly use personal pronouns, the definite article, demonstrative pronouns and adjectives, and connectors, your paragraph has good cohesion.

   a. true   **b.** false

II REVIEWING IDEAS

For each paragraph on pages 92–93, answer the following questions. Write your answers to questions 1, 2, and 3 on the lines below each paragraph. Mark your answer to questions 4 and 5 on the paragraph.

1. What kind of paragraph is it?
2. Does the paragraph have coherence? What kind?
3. Does the paragraph have unity?
4. Cross out any irrelevant sentence that you find.
5. Circle all the cohesive devices in the paragraph.

Paragraph 1

Holidays

In the United States, as in other countries, there are basically three types of holidays. The first group of holidays began as pagan[1] festivals[2]. An example of this is Halloween. This holiday began many centuries ago in Ireland and England. People lit fires and dressed up in costumes to scare bad spirits[3] away. I always like to see all the children in their Halloween costumes when they come to my house for trick-or-treating. The second type of holiday celebrates important historical or political events. Examples of these holidays are Memorial Day and Independence Day, also called the Fourth of July. Memorial Day honors the soldiers who died in American wars, and Independence Day celebrates the signing of the Declaration of Independence in 1776. The third and last category of holidays includes all of the holidays that have religious beginnings. A very common holiday of this type is Christmas. In short, holidays are celebrated for pagan, historical, and religious reasons.

[1] **pagan** *adj.* relating to an old religion that isn't one of the world's main modern religions

[2] **festival** *n.* a big party

[3] **spirit** *n.* a ghost

1. _____

2. _____

3. _____

Paragraph 2

The First Woman Doctor

Elizabeth Blackwell, the first woman doctor in the United States, had an extraordinary life for a nineteenth century woman. She was born in Bristol, England, in 1821. When she was eleven years old, she moved to New York City. After she finished university, she went to Geneva Medical School in Geneva, New York. She graduated from medical school in 1849, but she couldn't get a job in a hospital because she was a woman. As a result, she opened her own hospital in 1853. While she was working at this hospital, she opened the Women's Medical College in 1868. After that, she went home to England. Later, she helped in opening the London School of Medicine for Women in 1875. Finally, she died thirty-five years later in Hastings, England. In conclusion, Elizabeth Blackwell's life was unusual, but it was probably satisfying.

1. _____
2. _____
3. _____

III ERROR ANALYSIS

*Five sentences are correct. Put **C** next to those sentences. The other five are incorrect. Put **I** next to those sentences. Then correct the mistakes. Make sure the sentences have the correct punctuation.*

C 1. We leave three weeks from now.

          He called
I 2. ~~Called~~ her on her cell phone.

_____ 3. We found the cat on top of the house.

_____ 4. Harry's favorite actor Brad Pitt.

_____ 5. Until she finished her homework Lily didn't leave the library.

_____ 6. My children love stories. Therefore, I tell them lots of fairy tales.

_____ 7. Most Americans speak only English.

_____ 8. Margaret got divorced last year and she says she will never marry again.

_____ 9. Many people meet online before they go out on a date.

_____ 10. My parents still in love.

PART IV

OTHER TYPES OF PARAGRAPHS

CHAPTER 10: PROCESS

CHAPTER 11: REASONS AND RESULTS

CHAPTER 12: OPINION

PROCESS

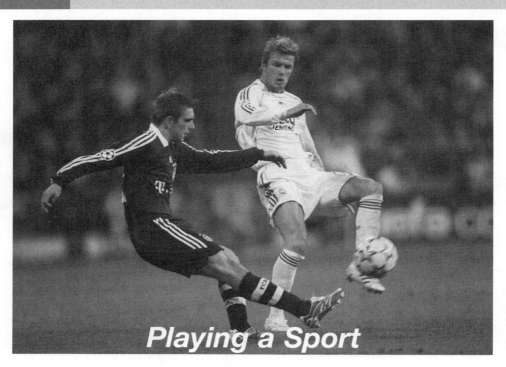

Playing a Sport

I VOCABULARY BUILDER

A. *Which of these sports do you know? Put a checkmark (✓) next to them. Add your favorite sports to the list.*

❑ baseball

❑ basketball

❑ soccer

❑ tennis

_____

_____

_____

_____

_____

_____

B. *Ask a classmate the following questions about your favorite sport. Discuss his or her answers.*

1. Where do people play [your favorite sport]?

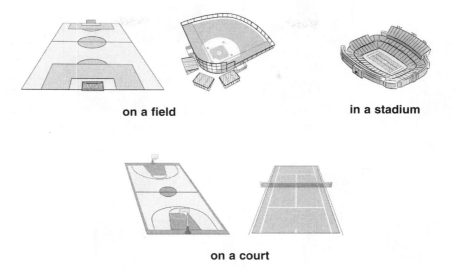

on a field   **in a stadium**

on a court

2. What equipment do the players need?

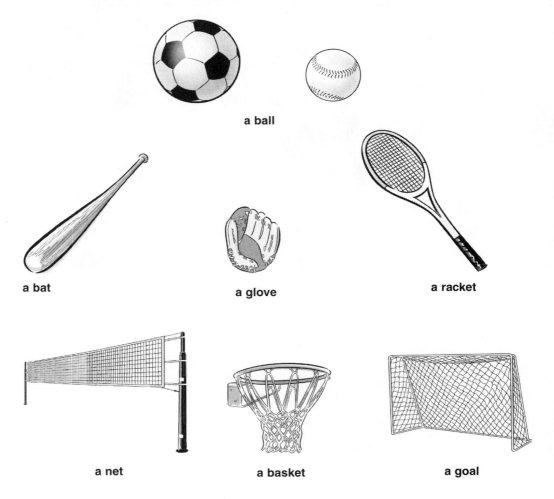

a ball

a bat   **a glove**   **a racket**

a net   **a basket**   **a goal**

3. What do the players do in your favorite sport?

throw catch dribble

jump pitch hit

serve run kick

Process

Process is a type of paragraph that explains how to do something. In a process paragraph, you usually write about the **steps** involved in doing something. Naturally, when you talk about steps, you list them in the order that you want the reader to do them. This always follows **time order**. Read this paragraph. Then, do Practice 1.

Model Paragraph 1

What about you?

Do you play soccer? What other sports do you like? Discuss this with a classmate.

Learning to Kick a Soccer Ball

Learning to kick a soccer ball well takes a lot of time. First, sit on the ground with your knees up. With your bare [1] foot, kick the ball up with the top of your foot. Be sure that your ankle is locked [2] and that your toes are pointed. Do this until you can kick the ball up two feet and catch it on the top of your foot. Next, stand up, and do the same thing. Try to kick the ball up six or seven feet, catch it with your foot, and balance [3] the ball on your foot. After that, kick the ball against a wall. Practice this many, many times. Finally, put your shoes on and go through the same three steps. In short, if you spend lots of time and follow these steps, you will know how to kick a soccer ball well.

---

[1] **bare** *adj.* without clothes or shoes

[2] **locked** *adj.* kept in one position

[3] **balance** *v.* to put something into a steady position without falling to one side or the other

---

■ PRACTICE 1: **Analyzing the Model Paragraph**

1. What is the topic in the topic sentence?
2. What is the controlling idea?
3. How many steps are there?
4. Can you easily follow the steps? Are any steps missing?
5. How many major supporting sentences are there?
6. What words tell you that the sentences are major supporting sentences?

Transitions in a Process Paragraph

The words that signal the different steps in a process paragraph are **transitions of time order.** These are the same type of transitions that are used in a narrative paragraph. See page 79 for a list of these transitions.

■ PRACTICE 2: **Ordering Supporting Sentences**

Put the sentences in each group in the correct time order. Write the numbers 1, 2, 3, etc., in the blanks.

1. Serving a tennis ball

    _____ Bring the racket forward and hit the ball.

    _____ Raise the racket directly over your head.

    _____ Keep your eye on the ball.

    _____ Toss the ball about three inches higher than the racket.

    __*1*__ Hold the ball.

    _____ Lower your racket in front of you.

    _____ When your arm is stretched as high as it can be, toss the ball up.

2. Hitting a baseball

    _____ After the pitcher throws the ball, wait for the ball to come to you.

    _____ Hold the bat as high as your shoulder.

    _____ Drop the bat and run to first base.

    _____ When the ball reaches you, swing the bat.

    _____ Make contact with the ball.

    _____ Place your feet shoulder-width apart.

    _____ Watch for the ball.

    _____ Stand in front of the plate.

Using the Imperative

When you write a process paragraph, you are telling someone how to do something. The **imperative** is usually the form of the verb that is used to do this. This imperative form is the verb without the subject *you*. Look at these sentences.

➤ **Kick** the ball.

➤ **Run** fast.

➤ **Stand** still.

These sentences look like they are fragments because they don't have a subject, but they are not. The subject *you* is hidden.

➤ (You) **kick** the ball.

➤ (You) **run** fast.

➤ (You) **stand** still.

Using the Negative Imperative

The negative of an imperative is formed by putting ***don't*** in front of the verb.

➤ **Don't kick** the ball.

➤ **Don't run** fast.

➤ **Don't stand** still.

The Imperative and Dependent Clauses

You can use the imperative in an independent clause, but you can't use the imperative in a dependent clause. Instead, you must use the subject *you* and the simple present form of the verb. Remember that a dependent clause is part of a complex sentence. It starts with a subordinating conjunction like *after, when,* or *before.*

➤ **Kick** the ball. Then, catch it with your foot.

➤ **After *you* kick** the ball, catch it with your foot.
   Dependent clause,   independent clause.

➤ **Run** faster. Then, you will win the race.

➤ **When *you* run** faster, you will win the race.
   Dependent clause,   independent clause.

➤ **Run** to first base. Hit the ball.

➤ **Before *you* run** to first base, hit the ball.
   Dependent clause,   independent clause.

■ PRACTICE 3: **Using the Imperative**

In the following paragraph, the pronoun *you* and several helping verbs are underlined. If they are not necessary, cross them out. Remember to use *don't* if the imperative is negative.

Becoming an Athlete

If <u>you</u> want to be an athlete, <u>~~you must~~</u> take good care of yourself. First, <u>you must</u> get enough exercise. After <u>you</u> exercise your heart and lungs by running, <u>you must</u> exercise your muscles by lifting weights. Second, <u>you should</u> eat right. <u>You must</u> eat a lot of fruits and vegetables and other foods high in protein and low in fat. You need calcium, so <u>you should</u> drink milk, too. Third, <u>you must</u> get enough sleep every night. For most people, this means sleeping at least seven or eight hours every night. Finally, if <u>you</u> drink alcohol and take drugs, your body will become weak. Therefore, <u>you should not</u> take them. In short, after <u>you</u> follow these suggestions, you will be on your way to becoming a good athlete.

 WRITING TO COMMUNICATE

Your Turn

Write a process paragraph about one of these topics. For additional help with the writing process, go to Appendix 1: *Going Through the Writing Process* on page 122.

1. Tennis: How to serve a ball. Use Practice 2 to help you.
2. Baseball: How to hit a ball. Use Practice 2 to help you.
3. Your favorite sport: How to do one simple action.

Paragraph Checklist

Use this checklist when you are finished writing your paragraph. If you like, you can switch paragraphs with your classmate and check each other's paragraph.

1. I explained how to do something. ....❑
2. My paragraph has a clear topic sentence. ....❑
3. The steps in my paragraph are in time order. ....❑
4. My paragraph has a clear concluding sentence. ....❑
5. I used the imperative correctly. ....❑
6. I didn't use the imperative in dependent clauses. ....❑
7. I used commas correctly. ....❑

Writing to Communicate . . . More

Using the process pattern is very common in writing instructions for baking and cooking. The first step is about gathering the ingredients and utensils that you will need. Then, you can talk about the steps. Look at this model paragraph.

Model Paragraph 2

The Best Sandwich

It's easy to make a delicious peanut butter and banana sandwich. First, you need to gather some ingredients: whole wheat bread, chunky [1] peanut butter, and a banana. You'll also need a knife. Next, take two slices [2] of whole wheat bread out of the package. Then, using the knife, spread the slices with the chunky peanut butter. Next, peel [3] the banana and cut it lengthwise. Put the pieces of banana on one of the two slices of bread. Finally, close the sandwich and cut it in half. In short, making this kind of sandwich is not difficult.

[1] **chunky** *adj.* with little pieces of peanuts in the peanut butter

[2] **slice** *n.* a flat piece of bread, cut from a larger piece

[3] **peel** *v.* to take the skin off

For extra writing practice, write a process paragraph about how to prepare a favorite food of yours.

Exercising

I VOCABULARY BUILDER

A. Match the pictures with the verbs in the box.

a. ride	**c.** skate	**e.** jog	**g.** swim
b. jump	**d.** lift	**f.** ski	**h.** stretch

1. _h_

2. ____

3. ____

4. _____

5. _____

6. _____

7. _____

8. _____

B. *Match the pictures with the nouns in the box.*

a. exercise mat	**c.** jump rope	**e.** skates
b. weights	**d.** skis and boots	**f.** bicycle

1. _____

2. _____

3. _____

4. _____

5. _____

6. _____

Explaining with Reasons and Results

There are many ways of explaining something. You can explain by giving examples (Chapter 6) or instructions (Chapter 10). You can also explain by giving **reasons** or **results**.

Giving Reasons

When you support your topic sentence with reasons, you say why your topic sentence is true. Read this paragraph. Then, do Practice l.

Model Paragraph 1

Water Aerobics

Participating in water aerobics [1] is beneficial to your body for many reasons. First of all, water aerobics gets your heart beating fast. This is good because it makes your heart strong. It also sends blood throughout your body. Second, water aerobics builds up the strength in your muscles. It is harder to move through water than through air, so you have to work harder. Finally, water aerobics is good because it doesn't put a strain [2] on your joints [3]. The water supports your weight, so your joints don't receive the pressure of all your weight. In short, for these reasons, you should try water aerobics.

| [1] **aerobics** *n.* a very active type of physical exercise done to music, usually in a class | [2] **strain** *n.* a situation in which something is being pulled, stretched, or pushed | [3] **joint** *n.* a part of the body where two bones meet that can bend |

> **What about you?**
>
> What type of exercise do you enjoy? Discuss your answer with a classmate.

■ PRACTICE 1: Analyzing Model Paragraph 1

1. What is the topic of this paragraph? Circle it.
2. What is the controlling idea of this paragraph? Underline it.
3. How many reasons are given to support the topic sentence?
4. What transitions begin each major supporting sentence? Put a box around them.
5. Add the correct number of minor supporting sentences.

> Major Supporting Sentence
>> Number of minor supporting sentences: _____
>
> Major Supporting Sentence
>> Number of minor supporting sentences: _____
>
> Major Supporting Sentence
>> Number of minor supporting sentences: _____

Giving Results

An event often causes certain results. In other words, results follow events. Read this paragraph. Then, do Practice 2.

Model Paragraph 2

> **A Positive Mind**
>
> There are very positive mental results to exercising. First, you will feel less stress [1]. Exercising reduces stress because you forget about your problems while you are exercising. Second, you will feel better about everything. Exercising releases [2] endorphins into your body. Endorphins are chemicals that make you feel good. Third, you will sleep better. Exercising helps you relax, so you can fall asleep more quickly and stay asleep longer. After sleeping well, you feel better throughout the next day. Finally, you will feel better about yourself. This will give you more confidence [3] to handle your daily life and even enjoy it. In conclusion, reducing stress, feeling good, sleeping better, and having more confidence are the positive results of exercising.

[1] **stress** *n.* continuous feelings of worry about your work or personal life that prevent you from relaxing

[2] **release** *v.* to stop holding something

[3] **confidence** *n.* a belief in your ability to do things well

What about you?

Do you agree that exercising helps your mind? Discuss this topic with your classmate.

■ PRACTICE 2: **Analyzing Model Paragraph 2**

1. What is the topic of this paragraph? Circle it.
2. What is the controlling idea of this paragraph? Underline it.
3. How many results are given to support the topic sentence?
4. What transitions begin each major supporting sentence? Put a box around them.
5. Add the correct number of minor supporting sentences.

   Major Supporting Sentence
      Number of minor supporting sentences: _____

   Major Supporting Sentence
      Number of minor supporting sentences: _____

   Major Supporting Sentence
      Number of minor supporting sentences: _____

   Major Supporting Sentence
      Number of minor supporting sentences: _____

Connectors for Reason and Result

To show reason and result, you can use three types of connectors: transitions, coordinating conjunctions, and subordinating conjunctions. The following charts list the most common connectors for reason and result. Study how they are used.

Transitions		
[Reason].	**Therefore,**	[result].
[Reason].	**As a result,**	[result].

Coordinating Conjunction
[Reason]**, so** [result].

Subordinating Conjunctions	
Because [reason], [result].	**Since** [reason], [result].
[Result] **because** [reason].	[Result] **since** [reason].

Study these sentences. Circle the connector.

➤ There was a big snowstorm. Therefore, we couldn't go skiing.
    reason   result

➤ Jimmy lifts weights. As a result, he is very strong.
    reason   result

➤ Lifting weights can be dangerous, so be careful.
    reason   result

➤ Yoga is good for you because it stretches your muscles.
    result   reason

➤ Water aerobics is good for Dad since it protects his joints.
    result   reason

■ PRACTICE 3: Using Connectors of Reason and Result

Combine the two sentences. Use the connector in parentheses. Make sure the reason and the result are in the correct place and punctuate correctly.

1. Jack prefers playing team sports. He likes being with other people.

   (because) _Jack prefers playing team sports because he likes being with other people._

   (therefore) _Jack likes being with other people. Therefore, he prefers playing team sports._

   (so) _____

2. Sebastian wants to get stronger. He is going to join a health club.

   (so) _____

   _____

   (since) _____

   _____

   (as a result) _____

   _____

3. Ivana practices yoga every day. She is very flexible.

   (as a result) _____

   _____

   (so) _____

   _____

   (because) _____

   _____

4. Dark chocolate is healthy. Ed only buys dark chocolate.

   (so) _____

   _____

   (since) _____

   _____

   (therefore) _____

   _____

Reviewing Types of Sentences

The three types of connectors you have studied result in different types of sentences.

Simple Sentences

You know that a **simple sentence** is one independent clause. It has a subject and a verb.

➤ John was sick.
Independent clause.

When you add a transition to the beginning of a simple sentence, it stays a simple sentence.

➤ John was sick. He couldn't go skiing.
Simple sentence.   Simple sentence.

➤ John was sick. **Therefore,** he couldn't go skiing.
Simple sentence.   Simple sentence.

Compound Sentences

When you combine two simple sentences with a coordinating conjunction, the combined sentence is a **compound sentence**.

➤ John was sick. He couldn't go skiing.
Simple sentence.   Simple sentence.

➤ John was sick, **so** he couldn't go skiing.
Compound sentence.

In other words, a compound sentence is two independent clauses connected by a coordinating conjunction.

➤ John was sick, **so** he couldn't go skiing.
Independent clause,   independent clause.

Complex Sentences

When you combine two simple sentences with a subordinating conjunction, the combined sentence is a **complex sentence**.

➤ John was sick. He couldn't go skiing.
Simple sentence.   Simple sentence.

➤ **Because** John was sick, he couldn't go skiing.
Complex sentence.

➤ John couldn't go skiing **because** he was sick.
Complex sentence.

In short, a complex sentence is one independent clause and at least one dependent clause.

➤ **Because** John was sick, he couldn't go skiing.
Dependent clause,   independent clause.

➤ John couldn't go skiing **because** he was sick.
Independent clause   dependent clause.

Read each sentence. Then, check (✓) the type of sentence it is.

1. Susana swims every day after she finishes work.
   ❏ simple   ❏ compound   ❏ complex

2. Good soccer players are very fast.
   ❏ simple   ❏ compound   ❏ complex

3. Hannah broke her tennis racket, so she bought a new one.
   ❏ simple   ❏ compound   ❏ complex

4. When George gets tired, he jumps rope for ten minutes.
   ❏ simple   ❏ compound   ❏ complex

5. You don't need to buy an exercise mat because I have an extra one.
   ❏ simple   ❏ compound   ❏ complex

6. I can use your skis, but your boots are too small.
   ❏ simple   ❏ compound   ❏ complex

7. Peter can lift a 100-pound weight over his head.
   ❏ simple   ❏ compound   ❏ complex

8. Until you get better, you shouldn't go swimming.
   ❏ simple   ❏ compound   ❏ complex

IV WRITING TO COMMUNICATE

Your Turn

Choose one of the following topics for a paragraph. To begin, find a classmate who is interested in the same topic. Take notes while you brainstorm together. Then, write your paragraph following the steps of the writing process. To review the writing process, see Appendix 1: *Going Through the Writing Process* on page 122.

1. What is your favorite form of exercise? Why is it your favorite?

2. Do you need a piece of sporting equipment for an exercise that you do? Which brand or type of this equipment is the best? Why?

3. What are the results to your body and mind if you don't exercise?

Paragraph Checklist

Use this checklist when you are finished writing your paragraph. If you like, you can switch paragraphs with your classmate and check each other's paragraph.

1 My paragraph has a clear topic sentence. . . . .☐

2 I supported my topic sentence by giving *(check one)*
   a. reasons. . . . .☐
   b. results. . . . .☐

3 The concluding sentence in my paragraph *(check one)*
   a. summarizes the major supporting sentences. . . . .☐
   b. restates the topic sentence. . . . .☐

4 I used *(check all that apply)*
   a. transitions. . . . .☐
   b. coordinating conjunctions. . . . .☐
   c. subordinating conjunctions. . . . .☐

5 I used *(write the number)*

   _____ simple sentences.

   _____ compound sentences.

   _____ complex sentences.

Writing to Communicate . . . More

For further practice writing paragraphs, choose one of the following types of exercise. Explain why people might get hurt doing this type of exercise.

- lifting weights
- riding a bike
- skating
- skiing

CHAPTER 12

OPINION

Discussing Movies

I VOCABULARY BUILDER

A. With a classmate, match the type of movie with the best description. Then, think of examples of each type of movie.

a. a story with surprises	**d.** a funny story
b. a story about two people falling in love	**e.** a scary story
c. a story about unbelievable things	**f.** a serious story

   d   **1.** a comedy   *Meet the Parents*

_____ **2.** a drama   _____

_____ **3.** a horror film   _____

_____ **4.** a romantic comedy   _____

_____ **5.** a science fiction film   _____

_____ **6.** a thriller   _____

B. *These adjectives in the box below can be used to describe movies. With a classmate, write each adjective in the correct column. If you don't know the meaning of an adjective, look it up in your dictionary. Think of other adjectives that can describe movies and write them in the appropriate column.*

4-star	boring	powerful	touching
awful	funny	terrible	wonderful

Positive   **Negative**

_____   _____

_____   _____

_____   _____

_____   _____

_____   _____

_____   _____

C. *Write a sentence about each of the movies you listed in Part A. Use one of the adjectives in the box above.*

1. *Meet the Parents was a funny movie.* _____

2. _____

3. _____

4. _____

5. _____

6. _____

Opinion Paragraphs

In an **opinion** paragraph, you write about what you think about a topic. Give your opinion in your topic sentence, and then support it with your supporting sentences that give **examples** or **reasons**.

Using Examples

Using examples is a good way to support your opinion. Use several examples to make your support as strong as possible. Read the following model paragraph. Then, do Practice 1.

Model Paragraph 1

Johnny Depp's Success

    In my opinion, Johnny Depp is a great actor because he has created so many memorable [1] characters. For example, in *Pirates of the Caribbean,* Depp created the very funny pirate, Captain Jack Sparrow. In *Charlie and the Chocolate Factory*, Depp was the weird [2] Willy Wonka, the man who didn't like children but loved chocolate. In *Finding Neverland*, Depp played James Barrie, the sweet, gentle man who wrote the children's book *Peter Pan*. In *Ed Wood*, it was almost impossible to recognize Depp as an actor because he was so good at being a bad director in the film. Of all the characters played by Johnny Depp, my favorite is Edward Scissorhands. Depp was perfect as the poor boy who had scissors for hands. In short, these are just a few of the roles that convinced [3] me that Johnny Depp is a wonderful actor.

> **What about you?**
>
> Who is your favorite actor or actress? Tell a classmate why you like him or her.

[1] **memorable** *adj.* very good or unusual, and worth remembering

[2] **weird** *adj.* unusual and very strange

[3] **convince** *v.* to make someone feel certain that something is true

■ **PRACTICE 1: Analyzing Model Paragraph 1**

1. What is the writer's opinion?
2. How many examples are there?
3. Do you think there are enough examples? Why or why not?
4. Are the examples convincing? Why or why not?

Using Reasons

You can also explain why you believe what you do by giving your reader the **reasons** why. In the following model paragraph, the writer explains his or her opinion by giving reasons. Read the paragraph. Then, do Practice 2.

Model Paragraph 2

The Most Successful Movie

In my view, *Titanic* is the most successful movie for good reasons. First, the story is based on a real one. When you watch the movie, you can experience the beauty of the ship *Titanic* and its tragic[1] ending. Second, the main characters in the movie, Jack and Rose, are played by very popular actors, Leonardo DiCaprio and Kate Winslet. Third, the story of these characters is gripping[2]. Jack is the poor man who falls in love with Kate and gives her a reason to live. However, they are together only for a little while. When the *Titanic* sinks, Jack dies, but their love does not. Most importantly, the special effects[3] are fantastic. When the ship sinks and Jack and Rose go down with it, you can almost feel their fear. In conclusion, *Titanic* was a success because of the real *Titanic*, the lead actors, the story of the main characters, and the visual effects.

[1] **tragic** *adj.* very sad and shocking

[2] **gripping** *adj.* holding all your attention and interest

[3] **special effects** *n.* unusual images produced artificially

■ **PRACTICE 2: Analyzing Model Paragraph 2**

1. What is the writer's opinion?
2. How many reasons are there?
3. Do you think there are enough reasons? Why or why not?
4. Are the reasons convincing? Why or why not?

Transitions for Opinion Paragraphs

There are two sets of transitions that can be used with opinion paragraphs: **transitions of opinion** and **transitions for order of importance**.

Transitions of Opinion

As you know, your opinion is stated in the topic sentence of your paragraph, so you don't always need a transition of opinion. If you want to emphasize that it is *your* opinion, you can start your topic sentence with one of these transitions.

Transitions of Opinion	
In my opinion, . . .	In my view, . . .

Transitions for Order of Importance

When you write an opinion paragraph and support it with **examples** or **reasons**, it is a good idea to present them by **order of importance**. Usually, writers put the most important example or reason last so that the reader will remember it. To convince the reader, you want him or her to remember your most important supporting idea.

Transitions for Order of Importance		
Above all, . . .	Most importantly, . . .	Most of all, . . .

III STRUCTURE AND MECHANICS

Avoiding Run-on Sentences

In Chapter 8, you learned about fragments, a common mistake. Another kind of common mistake in writing is to have two independent clauses separated by only a comma or by nothing. This type of mistake is called a **run-on sentence**. (X = incorrect)

X Madonna is a very popular singer, she doesn't act well.
Independent clause,   independent clause.

X Depp is a talented actor he gets offered a variety of roles.
Independent clause   independent clause.

There are three easy ways to fix run-on sentences.

1. Using a period and a capital letter:

   ➤ Madonna is a very popular singer**.** **S**he doesn't act well.

   ➤ Depp is a talented actor**.** **H**e gets offered a variety of roles.

2. Using a transition:

   ➤ Madonna is a very popular singer. **However,** she doesn't act well.

   ➤ Depp is a talented actor. **Therefore,** he gets offered a variety of roles.

3. Using a coordinating conjunction:

   ➤ Madonna is a very popular singer**, but** she doesn't act well.

   ➤ Depp is a talented actor**, so** he gets offered a variety of roles.

■ PRACTICE 3: **Identifying Run-on Sentences**

*Decide if each item below is correct (**C**) or a run-on sentence (**RO**). Rewrite each run-on sentence, fixing it in one of the following ways:*

- Add a period and capital letter.
- Add a period and a transition + comma.
- Add a comma and a coordinating conjunction.

_RO_ **1.** Ang Lee directed *Hulk*, he also directed *Brokeback Mountain*.

Ang Lee directed Hulk. He also directed Brokeback Mountain. OR

Ang Lee directed Hulk. Moreover, he directed Brokeback Mountain. OR

Ang Lee directed Hulk, and he also directed Brokeback Mountain.

_C_ **2.** You can watch movies on your portable DVD player. You never have to be bored.

_____ **3.** Dramas with Robin Williams are great, his comedies aren't so good.

_____

_____

_____ **4.** Madonna is a singer she is also an actress.

_____

_____

_____ **5.** People like going to movies in December, many movies come out then.

_____

_____

_____ **6.** *Star Wars* made a lot of money. *Titanic* is the number one money-making movie.

_____

_____

_____ **7.** A lot of people don't like going to movie theaters they rent DVDs.

_____

_____

_____ **8.** *The Departed* was the best movie of 2007. *Crash* was the best movie of 2006.

_____

_____

Your Turn

With a classmate, discuss your favorite movies, actors, and directors. Choose one and write a paragraph about it.

1. If you choose a movie, give your opinion and support your opinion with reasons.
2. If you choose an actor or a director, give your opinion and support your opinion with reasons or examples.

For additional help with the writing process, go to Appendix 1: *Going Through the Writing Process* on page 122.

Paragraph Checklist

Use this checklist when you are finished writing your paragraph. If you like, you can switch paragraphs with your classmate and check each other's paragraph.

1. My topic sentence has a clear topic and controlling idea. ......❑
2. My topic sentence starts with a transition of opinion. ....❑
3. I supported my opinion by using (*check one*)
    a. examples. ....❑
    b. reasons. ....❑
4. I used order of importance, and my most important example or reason comes last. ....❑
5. There are no run-on sentences in my paragraph. ....❑

Writing to Communicate . . . More

For further writing practice, choose one of the topics below to write about.

1. Which is better in a foreign language movie—subtitles (translated dialogues printed over the movie) or dubbing (translated dialogues recorded by speakers of your language)? Why do you think so?
2. Do you think movies depend too much on special effects? Why or why not?
3. Do you think people will still go to movie theaters in twenty years? Why or why not?

I REVIEWING TERMS

Fill in each blank below with one of the words from the box.

examples	process	reasons	results	time order

1. In a _____ paragraph, the writer explains how to do something. The supporting sentences are in _____.

2. One way to support your opinion is to use _____.

3. When you tell *why*, you write about the _____. When you tell about what happens after something happens, you write about the _____.

II REVIEWING IDEAS

Look at the three topic sentences below. Read each supporting sentence in the box on page 121 and decide which topic sentence (1, 2, or 3) it belongs with. Then, write it on the correct line. Make sure the supporting sentences are in good order.

1. It's good to know how to make hot chocolate during the winter season.
   - First, *gather all the ingredients: cocoa, sugar, and milk.* _____
   - Second, _____
   - Third, _____
   - Next, _____
   - Then, _____
   - Last, _____

2. Eating chocolate can make you feel better.
   - For example, _____
   - In addition, _____
   - Finally, _____

3. In my view, Scharffen Berger makes the best chocolate bars in the world.
   - First of all, _____
   - Moreover, _____
   - Most importantly, _____

a. Chocolate gives you quick energy.

b. Combine 2 teaspoons of sugar with 1 teaspoon of cocoa.

c. Gather all the ingredients: cocoa, sugar, and milk.

d. Heat 1 cup of milk in a small pot slowly.

e. Just smelling the bar makes your mouth water.

f. Chocolate releases endorphins into your body.

g. Pour the chocolate mixture into the warming milk and stir.

h. Put 1 tablespoon of the warming milk into the sugar and cocoa mixture.

i. Chocolate makes you more alert.

j. Stir the milk until the sugar and cocoa mixture has melted.

k. The chocolate is smooth and melts in your mouth.

l. The taste of the chocolate is beyond belief.

III ERROR ANALYSIS

This paragraph has fifteen mistakes with capital letters, commas, and periods. Read the paragraph carefully and correct the mistakes.

Science fiction movies

In my opinion science fiction movies are the best type of movie. First of all, these movies give us glimpses[1] into the future. *The Matrix* movies are good examples of futuristic movies. In these movies. People experience life in a matrix[2] but it is in their minds only. Second, science fiction movies make us think about the future. Robots[3] do all the boring jobs in *AI: Artificial Intelligence,* they cook food clean houses and fix cars. However the robots make life for humans difficult. We must think about that future. Do we want a life like that? Most of all, movies about the future give us hope that humankind will survive,[4] a movie like *Children of men* show us a future that is miserable but it also shows us that we will survive. In conclusion, the greatest science fiction movies are about the future.

[1] **glimpse** *n.* a quick look

[2] **matrix** *n.* a situation from which a person or a society can grow

[3] **robot** *n.* a machine that can move and do some of the work of a person and is controlled by a computer

[4] **survive** *v.* to continue to live in spite of difficulties

When you need help writing a paragraph, use this worksheet to help you go through the steps of the writing process.

Step 1: Understanding the Assignment

Answer these questions.

1. What is my topic? _____

2. How much should I write? _____

3. When should I turn it in? _____

4. What format should I use? _____

5. Where do I get the information? _____

Step 2: Brainstorming

Use this space to make a list of all your ideas about your topic.

Step 3: Organizing Your Ideas

Look at all the ideas that you wrote above. Which ones go together? Narrow down your topic. What do you want to say about your topic? That is your controlling idea.

Topic: _____

Controlling Idea: _____

Topic Sentence: _____

Step 4: Writing the First Draft

Write your supporting sentences. Remember that the major supporting sentences should directly support your topic sentence. The minor supporting sentences should support the major supporting sentences. Use this outline as you write, but keep in mind that you may have more or fewer major supporting sentences and more or fewer minor supporting sentences.

TS _____

SS _____

    ss _____

    ss _____

SS _____

    ss _____

    ss _____

SS _____

    ss _____

    ss _____

Now, write your concluding sentence. Which type would be best for your paragraph? You can restate the topic sentence, or write a summary of the points in the supporting sentences.

CS _____

Take a break: If you have time, put this first draft aside for a little while.

Step 5: Rewriting

*First, **revise** your paragraph. Ask yourself these questions:*

- Is the paragraph well organized?
- Does the topic sentence have an opinion?
- Do the supporting sentences really support your topic sentence?
- Does your concluding sentence start with a transition?

*Next, **edit** your paragraph by checking for grammar, vocabulary, or spelling mistakes.*

Step 6: Writing the Final Draft

Write the final draft of your paper in the format that your teacher wants.

To check your work, go to Appendix 3: *A Complete Paragraph Checklist,* on page 127.

COMMON CONNECTORS

	Transitions	Coordinating Conjunctions	Subordinating Conjunctions	Prepositions	Adjectives

Space Order				to your right
				to your left
				above
				  (something)
				around
				behind
				below
				between
				  (two things)
				in
				in front of
				next to
				on
				under	

Time Order	first at first second third next then after that at last in the end finally	and	after before until when while		the first *(thing)* the second the third the next the last the final
Logical Order	first first of all second third next last last of all finally				the first *(thing)* the second the third the next the last the final

(continued)

COMMON CONNECTORS

	Transitions	Coordinating Conjunctions	Subordinating Conjunctions	Prepositions	Adjectives
Order of Importance	most of all above all more importantly				
Example	for example for instance as a (first, second, final) example				
Addition	also in addition moreover				
Opinion	in my opinion in my view				
Contrast	however	but			
Reason			because since		
Result	as a result therefore	so			
Conclusion	in conclusion in short				

CONTENT

1 My paragraph is *(check one)*
  a. descriptive. . . . . ❑
  b. narrative. . . . . ❑
  c. expository. . . . . ❑

2 My paragraph has unity. In other words, there are no
irrelevant sentences in my paragraph. . . . . ❑

ORGANIZATION

1 My topic sentence has a clear topic and a clear
controlling idea. . . . . ❑
Circle the topic. Underline the controlling idea.

2 The body of my paragraph has major supporting
sentences and minor supporting sentences. . . . . ❑

3 My paragraph has a concluding sentence. It is a *(check one)*
  a. restatement of the topic sentence. ❑
  b. summary of the major supporting sentences. . . . . ❑

STRUCTURE AND MECHANICS

1 I used good paragraph format. . . . . ❑

2 My paragraph has a title. . . . . ❑

3 All my sentences begin with a capital letter and end
with a period. . . . . ❑

4 I used the following connectors correctly *(check all that you used)*:
  a. transitions . . . . ❑
  b. coordinating conjunctions . . . . ❑
  c. subordinating conjunctions . . . . ❑

5 I used commas correctly with these connectors. . . . . ❑

Most teachers prefer that you type all writing assignments. Some even want you to turn in your paragraph by e-mail. It's important that you know how to format your paragraph on a computer. Here are some guidelines for doing this. Following the list of guidelines is a model paragraph.

1. Use a 12-point font. Common fonts used for academic writing are Times New Roman, Georgia, and Arial.

2. Put your name and date in the upper right-hand corner. You can also add the name of the course and the professor's name if you like.

3. Center your title by clicking on the centering icon. Return to left justification by clicking the icon.

4. Double-space the text by clicking on FORMAT. Then choose PARAGRAPH. Then choose LINE SPACING. Then choose DOUBLE.

5. Indent the first line of your paragraph by pressing the TAB key.

6. Capitalize the beginning of each sentence. Put one space between each word. DO NOT leave a space between the last word and the period.

7. DO NOT leave a space between a word and a comma.

8. Put one or two spaces between one sentence and the next one.

9. DO NOT press ENTER at the end of a line. The sentence will automatically go to the next line when the space is used up.

10. Red lines under a word indicate a misspelling. Correct the spelling.

11. Green lines indicate a grammar mistake. If you understand the suggested correction, then make the change. If you don't, leave your sentence as it is. Your teacher will explain it to you.

Model Paragraph

Min Hee Cho

February 14, 2008

English Writing 101

My Morning Routine

My morning routine during the week is always the same. My alarm clock rings at seven o'clock in the morning, and I usually get up at once. I jump out of bed and do exercises for about ten minutes. Then, I am ready to take a quick shower. After my shower, I plug in my electric toothbrush and brush my teeth. Next, I comb my hair. After that, I pick out my clothes for the day and get dressed. Then I eat breakfast. For breakfast, I usually have grapefruit juice, eggs, toast, and coffee. After breakfast, I sometimes listen to the news on the radio. At eight o'clock, I put on my coat and leave for work. In short, my mornings are boring, but that's the way I like them.

■ PRACTICE: **Typing a Paragraph on the Computer**

Type the following sentences in the order given on the computer. Use good paragraph format.

Title: Schools in the United States

Topic Sentence: There are five stages to American education.

Supporting Sentences: *(These sentences are in the correct order.)*

- The first stage is nursery school or pre-school.
- This is for children from ages three to five.
- Once a child reaches age five, he or she goes to elementary school.
- Usually, children go to elementary school for six years.
- Then, at ages eleven to twelve, children go to junior high school.
- Junior high school lasts for two or three years.
- After junior high school comes high school.
- Students begin this school at ages fourteen or fifteen.
- Students remain in high school for three or four years.
- After graduation from high school, students have the option of going on to college, where they could remain for any number of years.

Concluding Sentence: In short, children in the United States may go through nursery school, elementary school, junior high school, high school, and college.

PARAGRAPH EVALUATION

Content	**30–28**: great **27–24**: good **23–21**: OK, average **20–0**: needs improvement	• interesting to read; good ideas • excellent support • unified; no irrelevant sentences
Organization	**30–28**: great **27–24**: good **23–21**: OK, average **20–0**: needs improvement	• topic sentence with topic and controlling idea • major and minor supporting sentences • concluding sentence • good coherence • good use of cohesive devices
Structure	**20–18**: great **17–16**: good **15–14**: OK, average **13–0**: needs improvement	• correct grammar • correct words and word forms • good use of connectors
Mechanics	**20–18**: great **17–16**: good **15–14**: OK, average **13–0**: needs improvement	• good paragraph format • capital letters and periods used correctly • commas used correctly
Total	_____ Content + _____ Organization + _____ Structure + _____ Mechanics = _____ Total	• **100–90** = A • **89–80** = B • **79–70** = C • **69–60** = D • **59–0** = F

¶	Indent for paragraph.	
cap	Mistake in use of capital letter	$\overset{cap}{\text{(w)}}$e went to $\overset{cap}{\text{(c)}}$anada.
sp	Mistake in spelling	Don't $\overset{sp}{\text{(argu)}}$with me.
p	Mistake in punctuation	You're late $\overset{p}{\bigcirc}$
c	Mistake in comma use	I left $\overset{c}{\bigcirc}$ but she stayed.
poss	Mistake in possessive	I washed $\overset{poss}{\text{(the)}}$face.
wo	Wrong word order	He has a $\overset{wo}{\text{(shirt blue)}}$.
ww	Wrong word	The table is $\overset{ww}{\text{(tall)}}$.
wf	Wrong form of word	I enjoy $\overset{wf}{\text{(to ski)}}$.
ref	Unclear reference	Tom put $\overset{ref}{\text{(their)}}$books away.
t	Mistake in verb tense	He $\overset{t}{\text{(goes)}}$ yesterday.
prep	Mistake in preposition	He's married $\overset{prep}{\text{(with)}}$her.
art	Add an article.	Jim ate $\overset{art}{\wedge}$ banana.
agr	Mistake in verb agreement	Sue $\overset{agr}{\text{(know)}}$ how to dance.
#	Mistake in singular or plural	I have three $\overset{\#}{\text{(brother)}}$. I have one $\overset{\#}{\text{(sisters)}}$.
^	Add a word or words.	Six $\wedge$ an even number.
X	Eliminate this word.	The $\overset{X}{\text{my}}$ book is there.

frag	Fragment	*frag* 〈At the restaurant.〉
ro	Run-on sentence	*ro* 〈I saw the cat, it was black.〉
inf	Too informal for academic writing	*inf* The party was 〈cool.〉
?	Unclear	
OK	Teacher mistake. Ignore it.	

INDEX

adjectives, 21, 40, 44
    descriptive adjective, 7
    and the imperative, 101
    order of before nouns, 45
antecedent, 86

coherence, 74, 78
cohesion, 83
cohesive devices, 83
comma, 30, 50
complete sentence, 8
complex sentence, 50, 110
compound sentence, 30, 110
concluding sentence, 4, 26
connectors, 20, 70, 78, 84
    of reason and result, 108
controlling idea, 5
coordinating conjunctions, 30, 117

definite article, 84
demonstrative pronouns, 85
dependent clause, 50, 111
descriptive paragraphs, 38, 40, 75, 78

examples, 57, 114, 117
expository paragraphs, 57, 77, 78

fragments, 79

giving reasons, 106
giving results, 107

imperative, 101
impression, 40
independent clause, 29
irrelevant sentence, 69

linking verbs, 44
logical order, 57, 77, 78

narrative paragraphs, 49, 76, 78
nouns, 21

opinion, 7, 114

paragraph format, 9
personal pronouns, 85, 86
prepositions of place, 41
process, 99
punctuation, 8

reasons, 114, 116
restatement, 27
run-on sentences, 117

simple sentences, 29, 110
space order, 41, 74, 78
subordinating conjunctions, 51
summary, 27
supporting sentences, 4, 15
    major supporting sentences, 16, 17
    minor supporting sentences, 16, 17

time order, 50, 76, 78, 99
title, 10
topic, 5
topic sentence, 4, 5
transitions, 28, 117
    of example, 58
    of logical order, 58
    of opinion, 116, 117
    of time, 51
    of time order, 50, 99
    for order of importance, 116, 117

unity, 67

verb, 8, 21

writing process, 11, 22

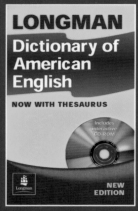

LONGMAN
Dictionary of American English

NOW WITH THESAURUS

Includes interactive CD-ROM

NEW EDITION

The perfect partner for
Writing to Communicate 1

1

Writing to Communicate

Paragraphs

Cynthia A. Boardman

With a combined process and product approach, *Writing to Communicate* puts students on a fast track to clear and effective academic writing.

Writing to Communicate 1 teaches students to write well-organized paragraphs in key rhetorical modes.

Features

- Theme-based chapters encourage students to explore ideas.
- *Vocabulary Builder* sections provide useful language for writing.
- Abundant and clear models give students solid support.
- Pair and group assignments promote collaborative learning.
- *Structure and Mechanics* sections develop accuracy.
- Paragraph checklists help students to revise their work.
- *Bringing It All Together* chapters provide opportunities for consolidation and assessment.

Writing to Communicate 1: Paragraphs	**0-13-614191-9**	**978-0-13-614191-4**
Writing to Communicate 1 Answer Key	0-13-614192-7	978-0-13-614192-1
Writing to Communicate 2: Paragraphs and Essays	0-13-235116-1	978-0-13-235116-4
Writing to Communicate 2 Answer Key	0-13-235115-3	978-0-13-235115-7

PEARSON
Longman

www.pearsonlongman.com

ISBN-13: 978-0-13-614191-4
ISBN-10:   0-13-614191-9

EAN

9 780136 141914

9 0000

T2-FQB-808